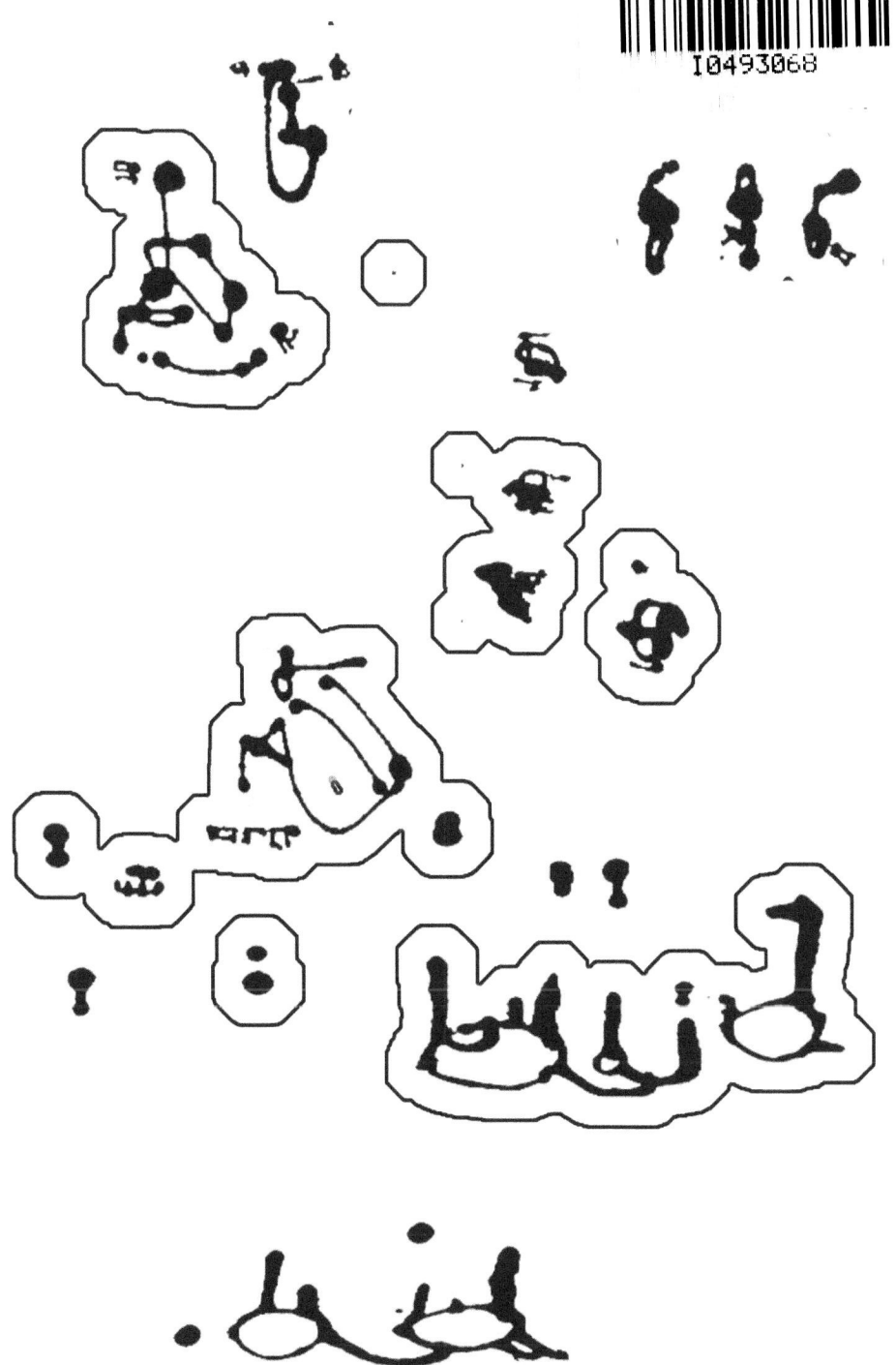

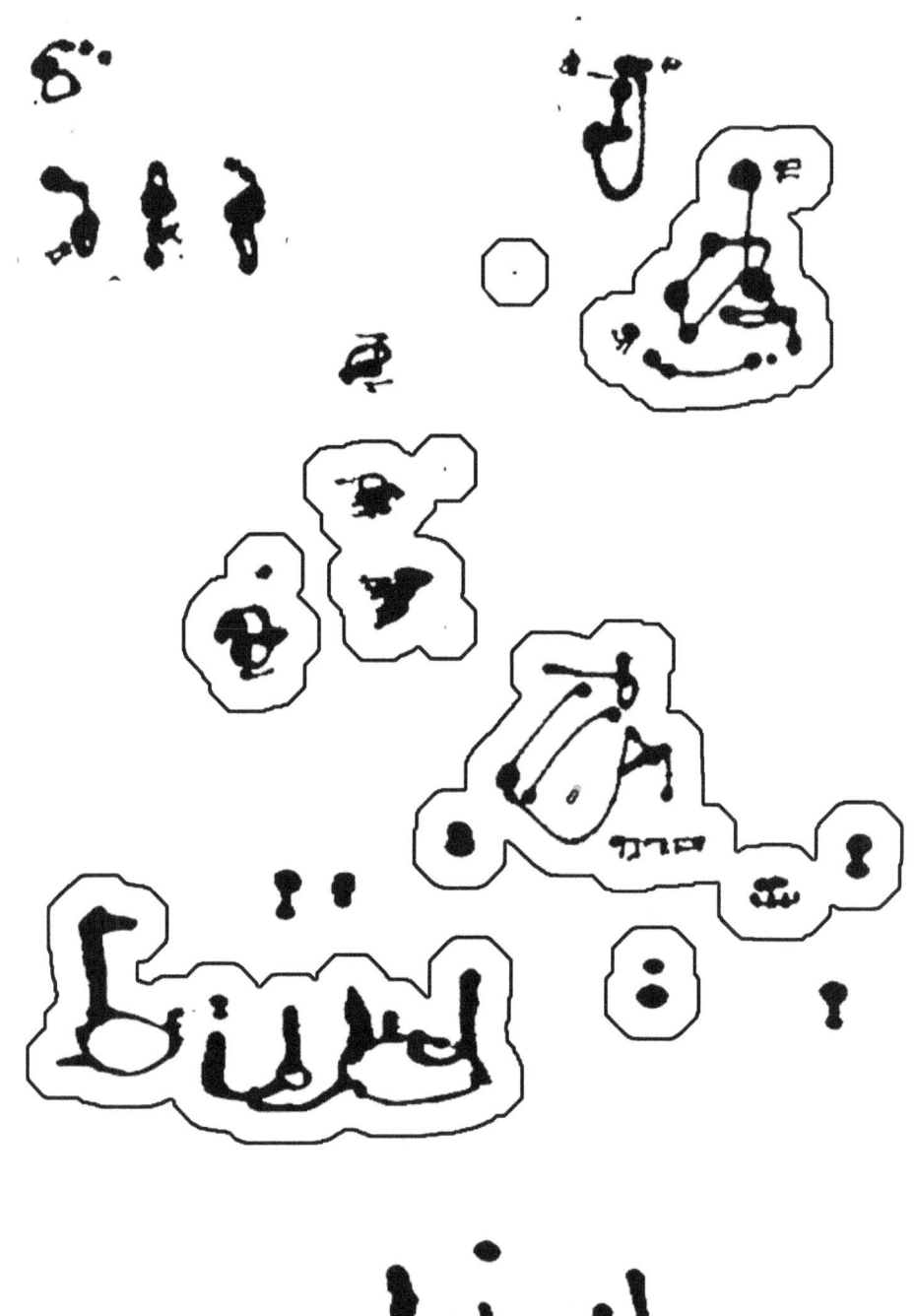

not-tulips
(visual haiku)

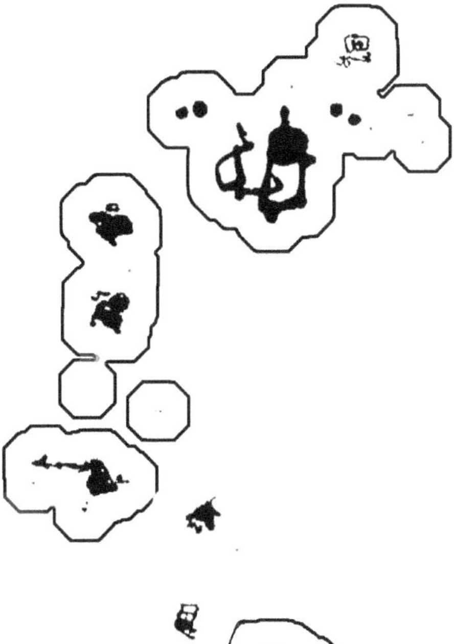

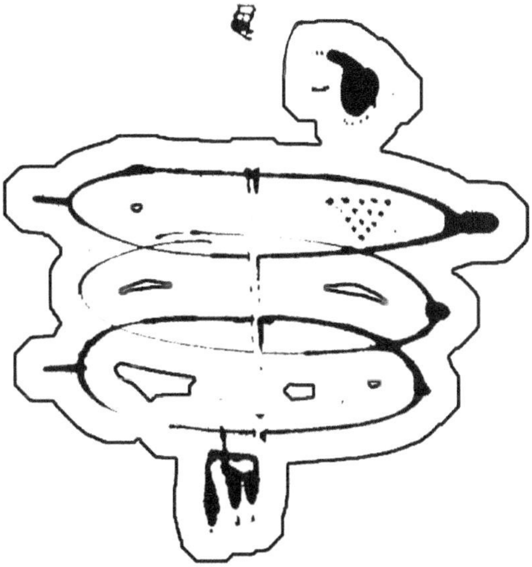

by

Rosaire Appel

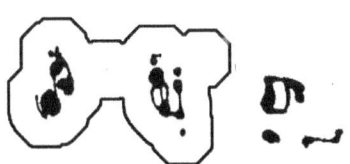

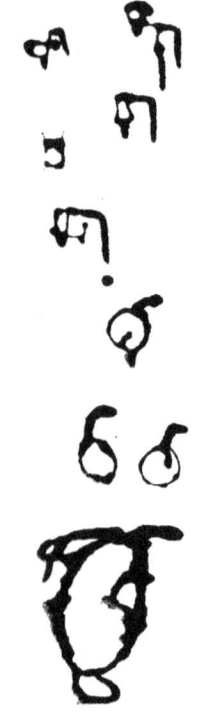

PRE^S_SRAPPEL

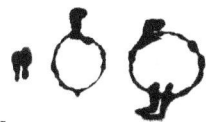

These are *not-tulips* – they
have no color, need no wa-
ter, won't wilt and die. . . .

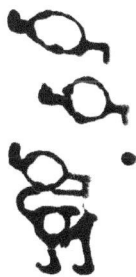

· · · perhaps they are
not haiku either.

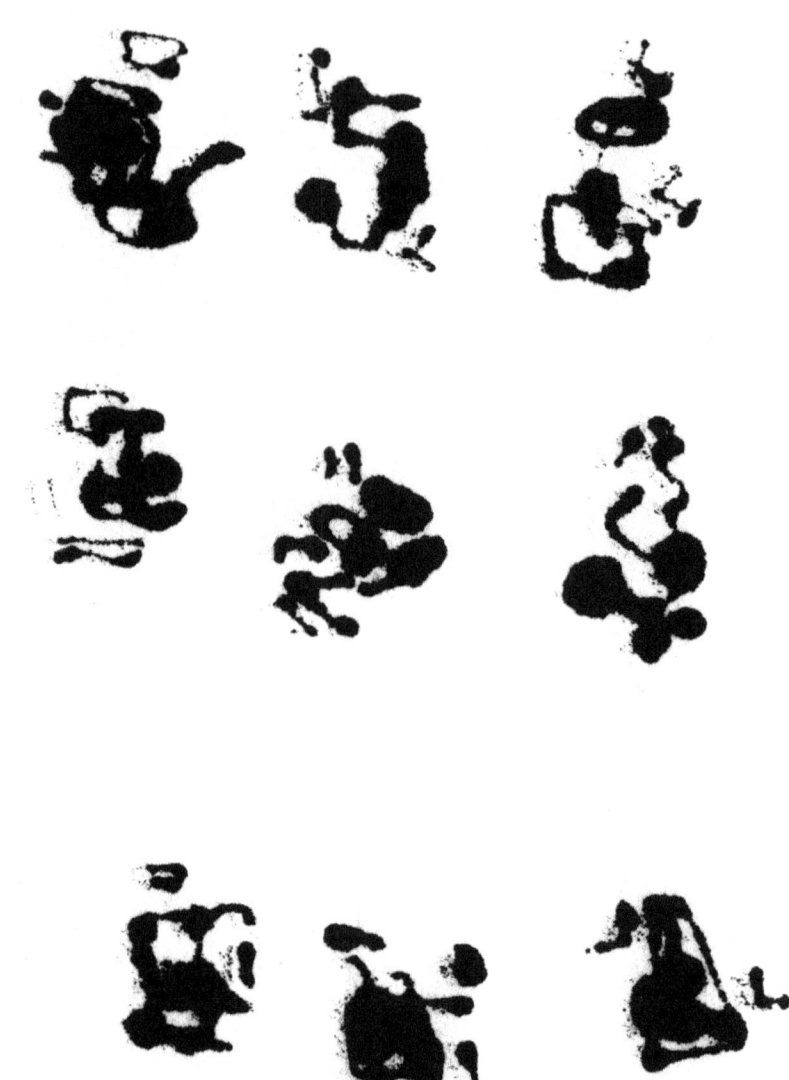

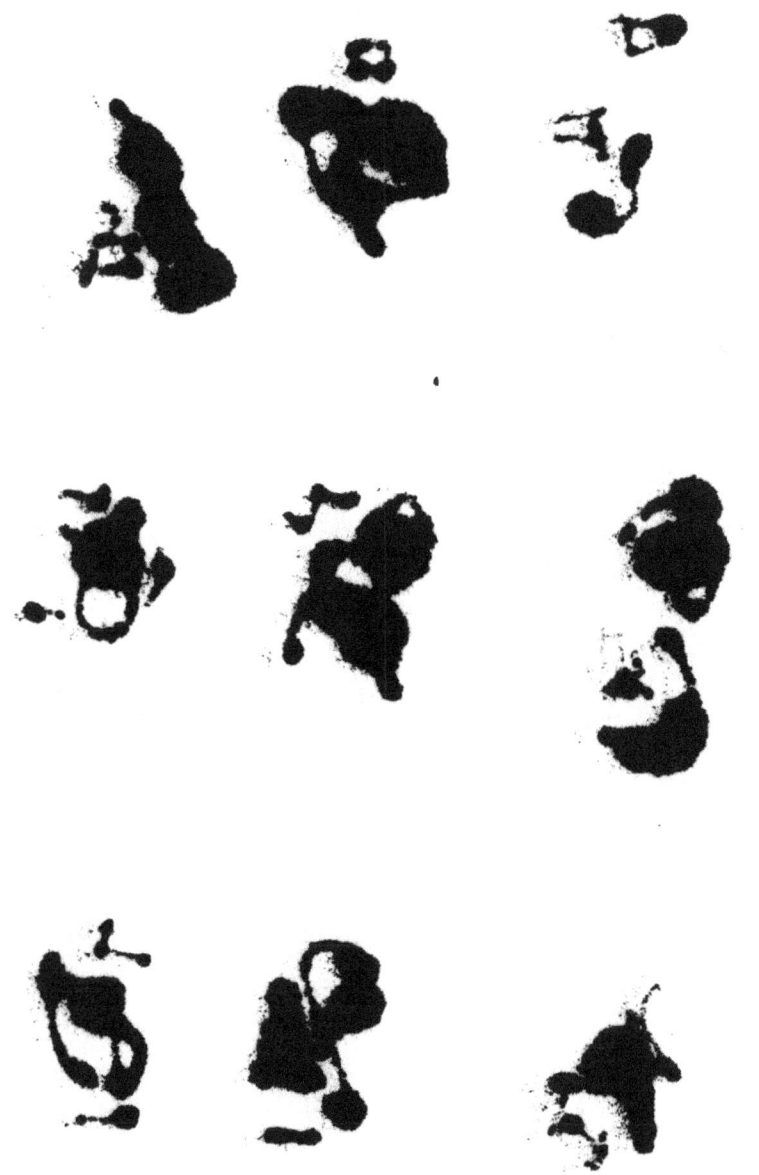

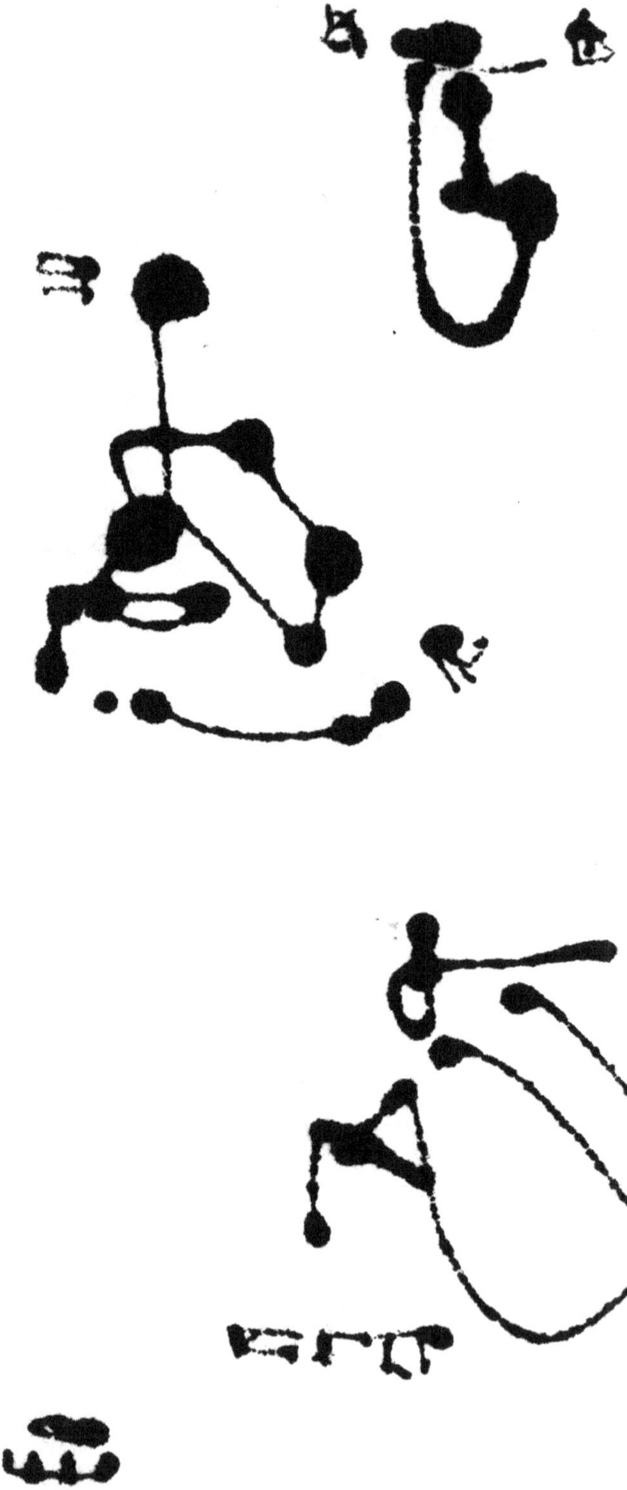

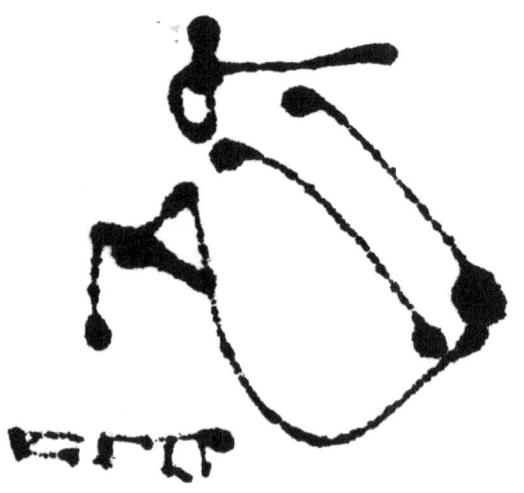

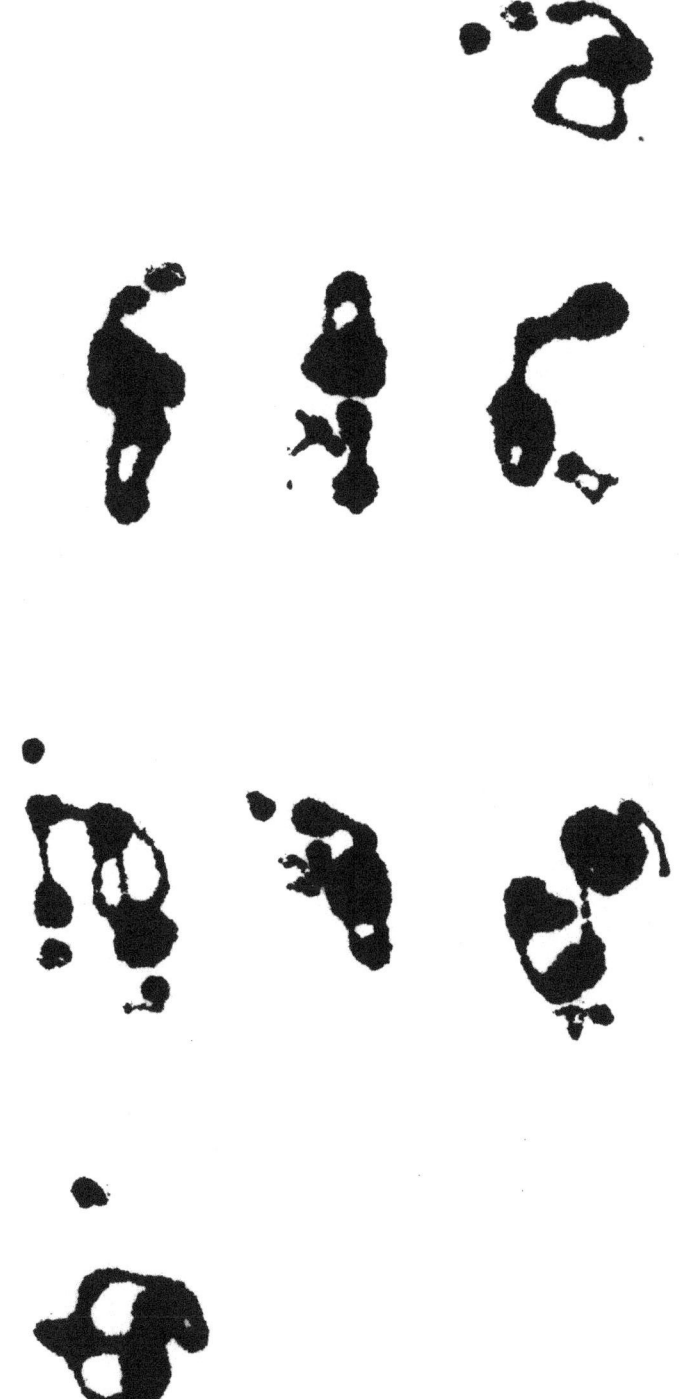

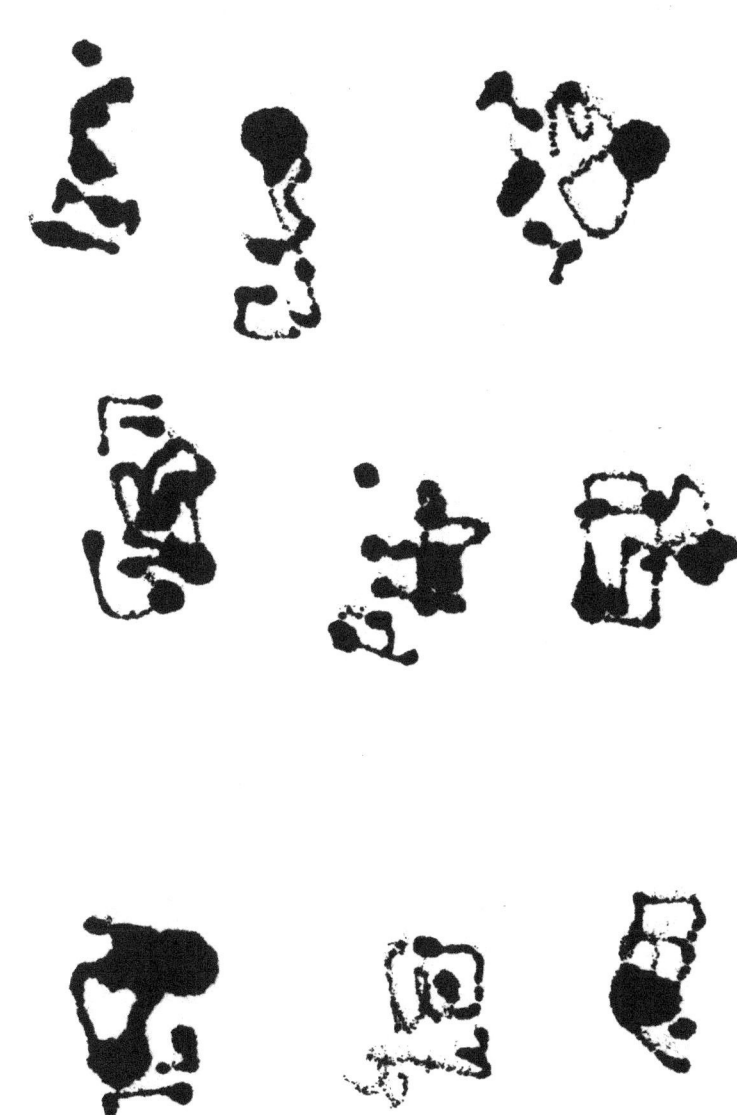

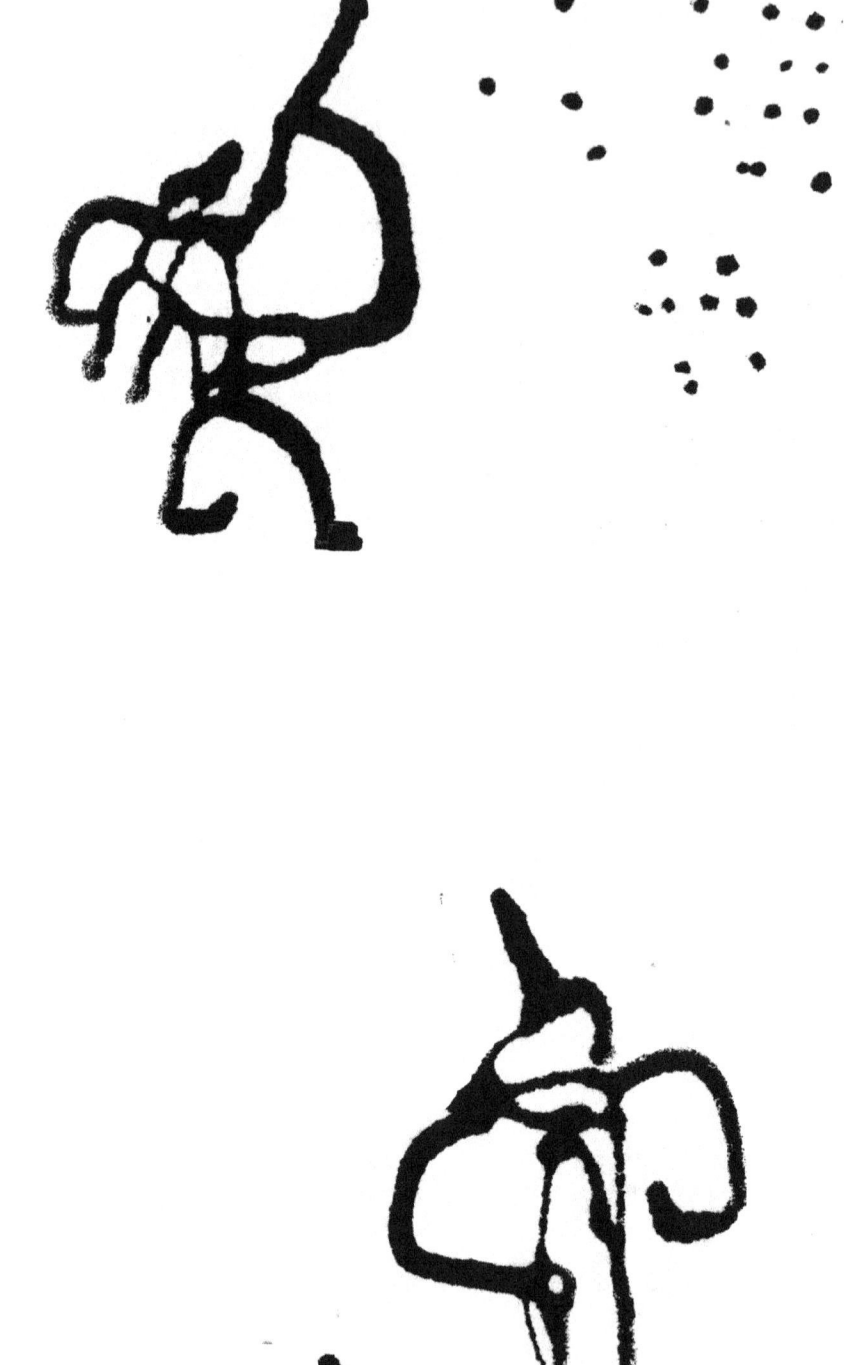

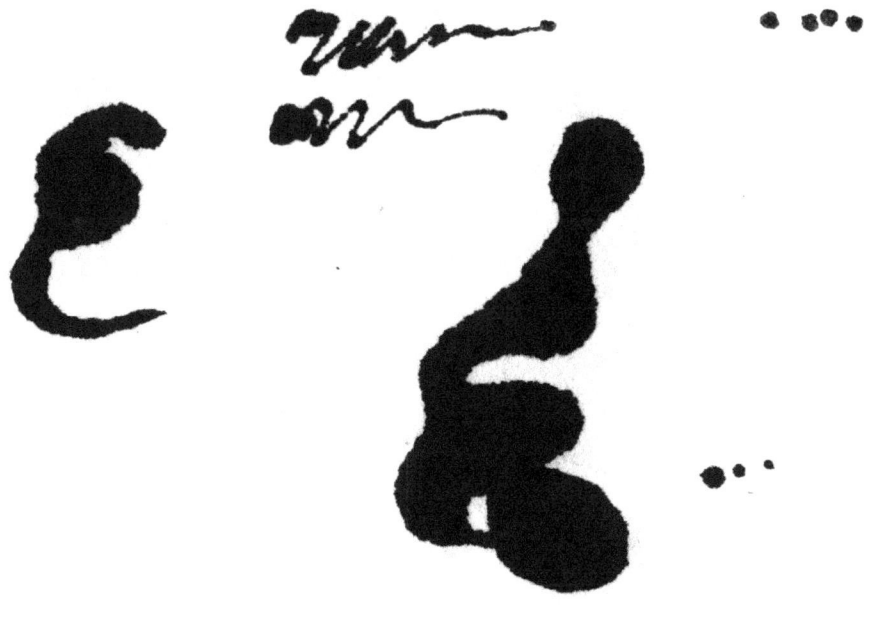

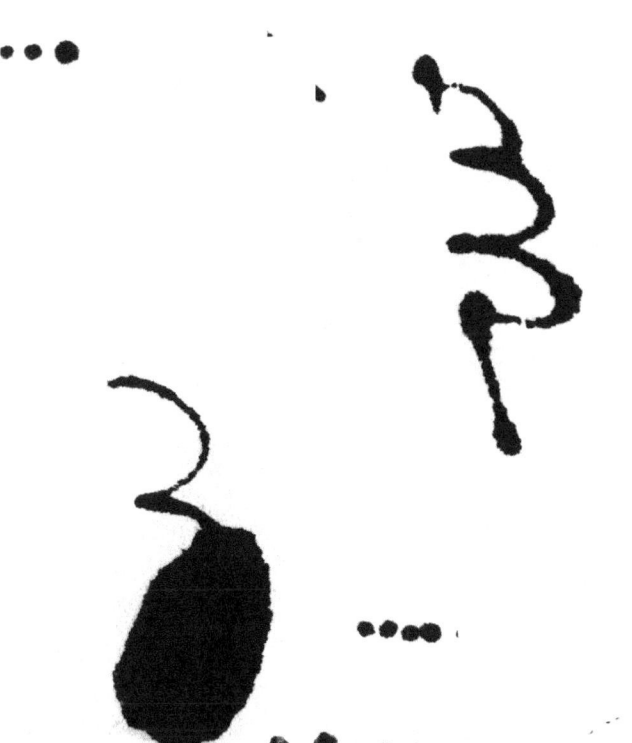

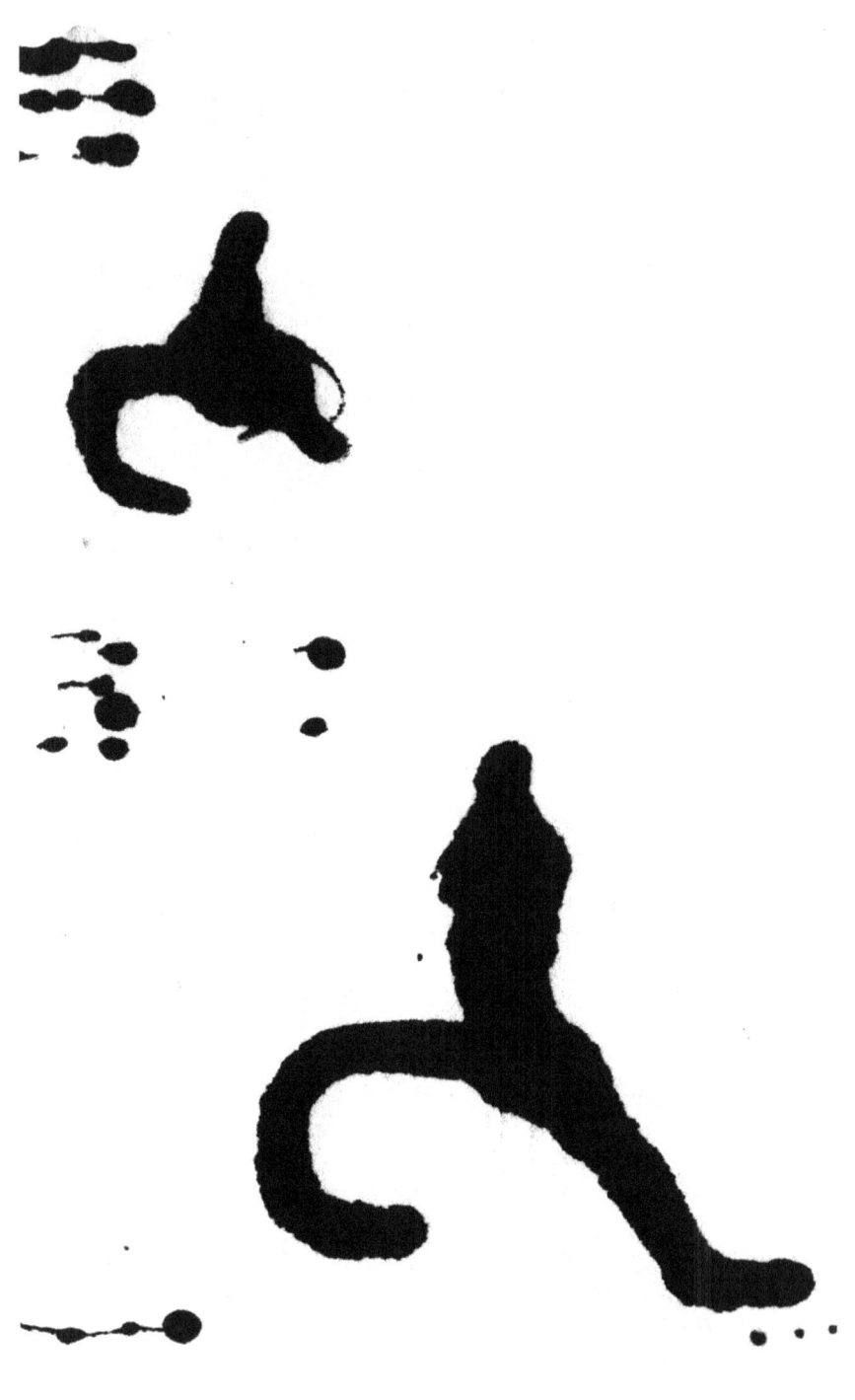

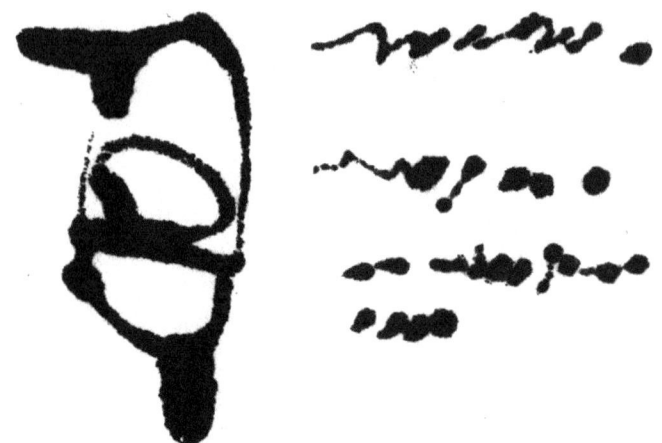

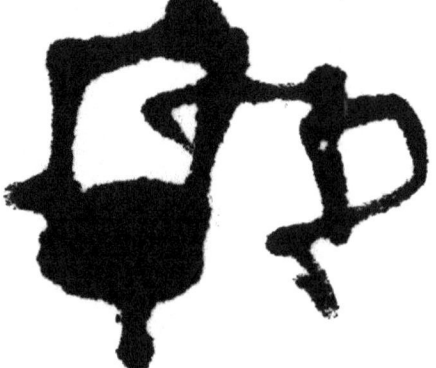

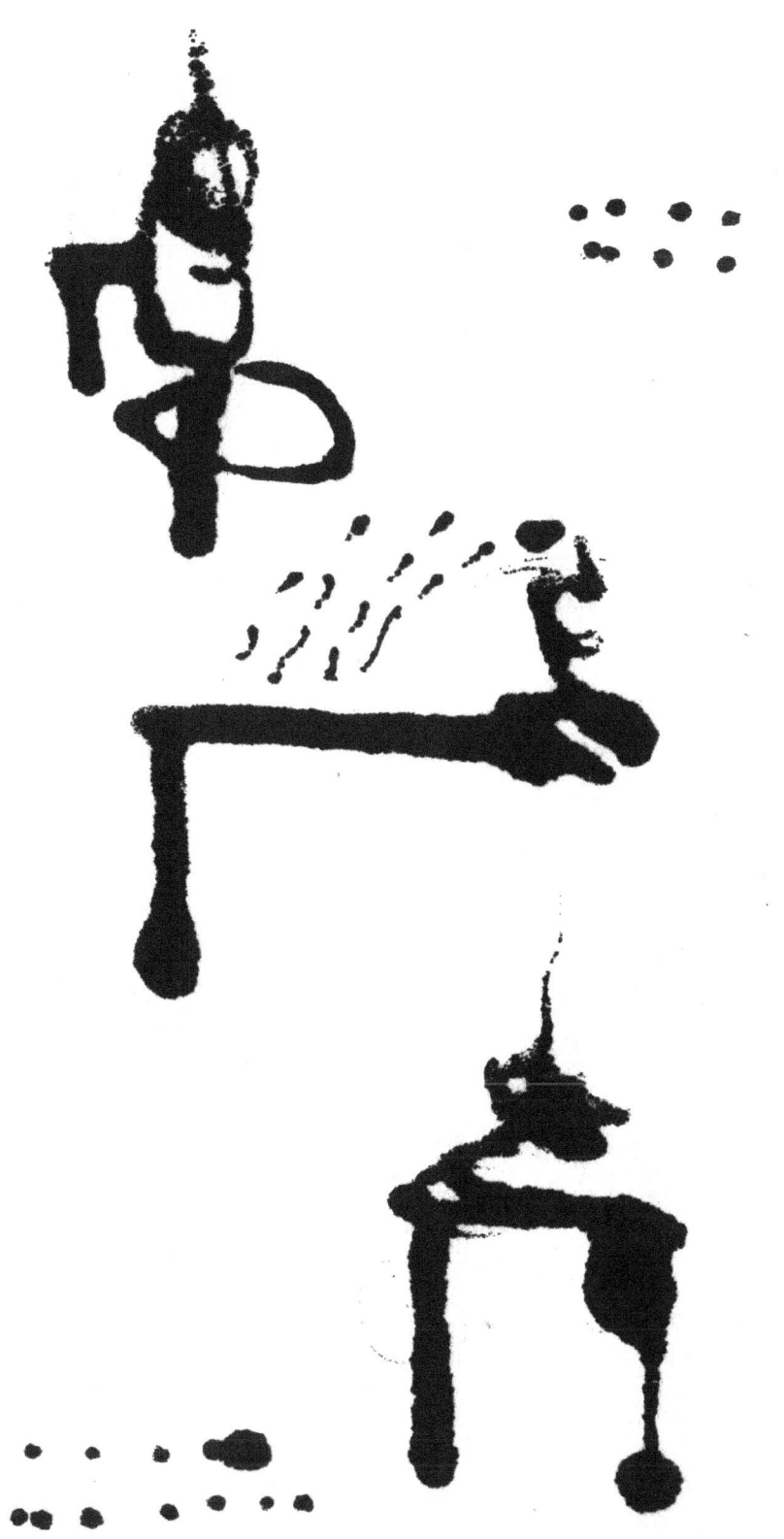

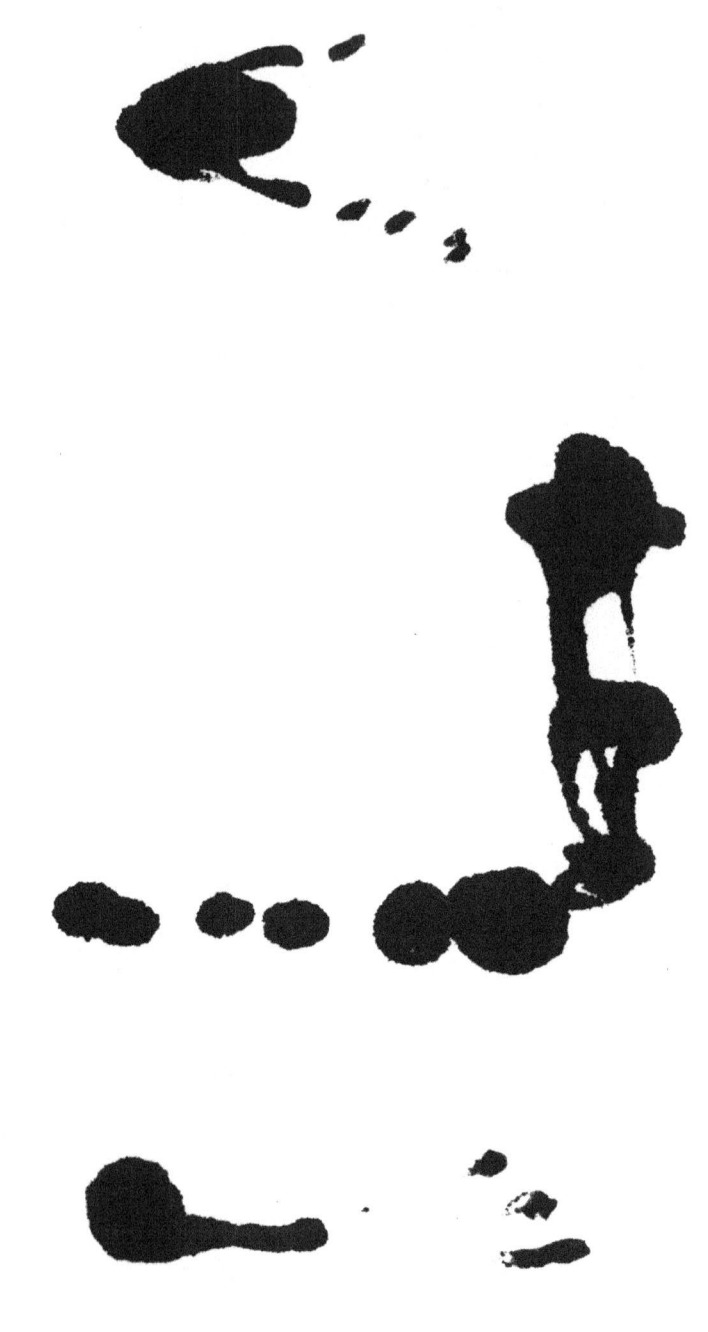

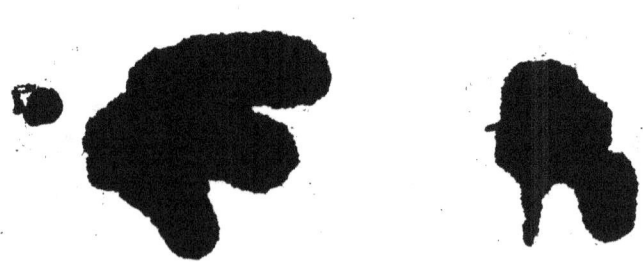

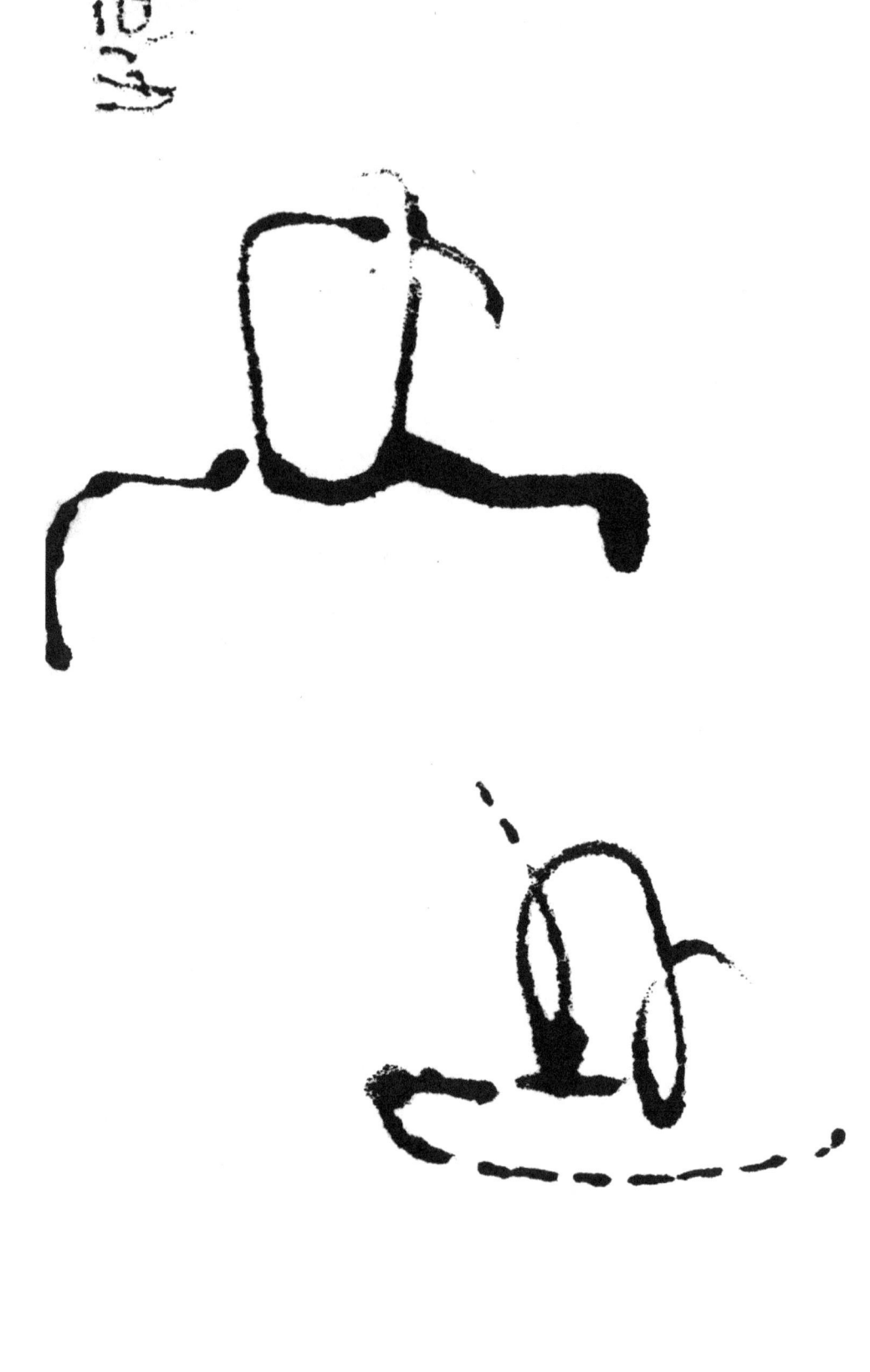

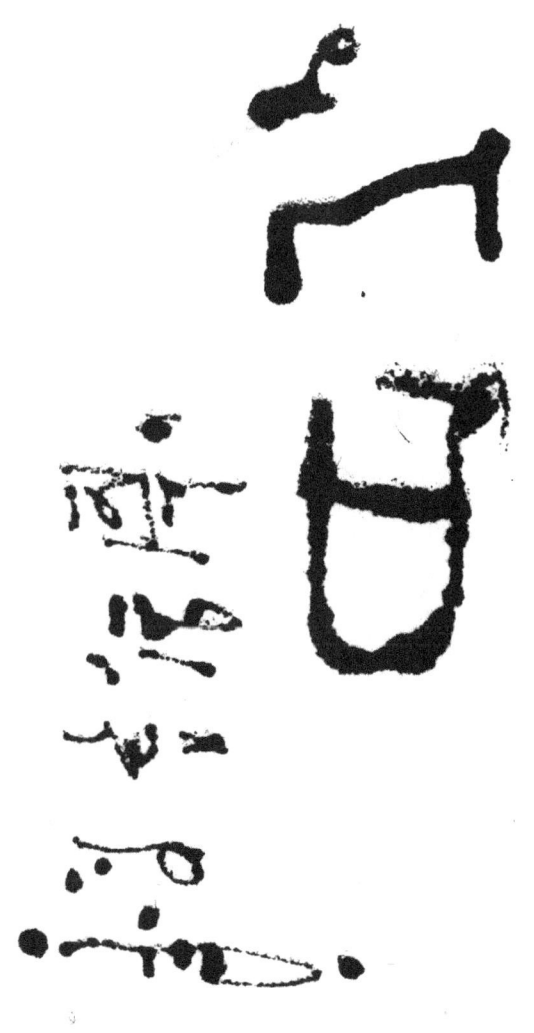

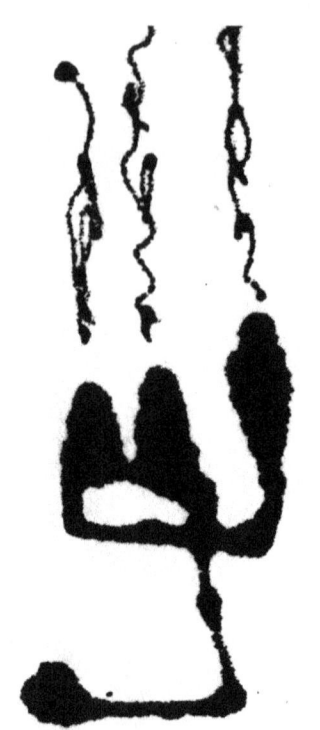

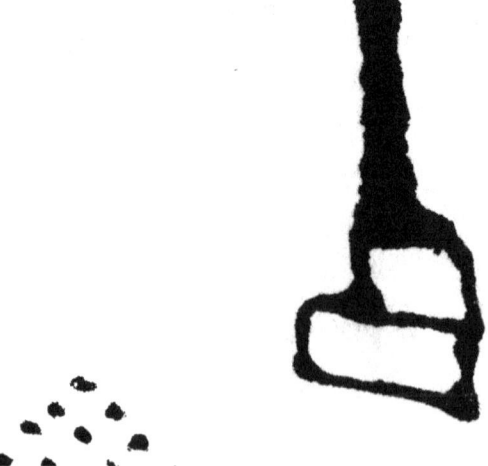

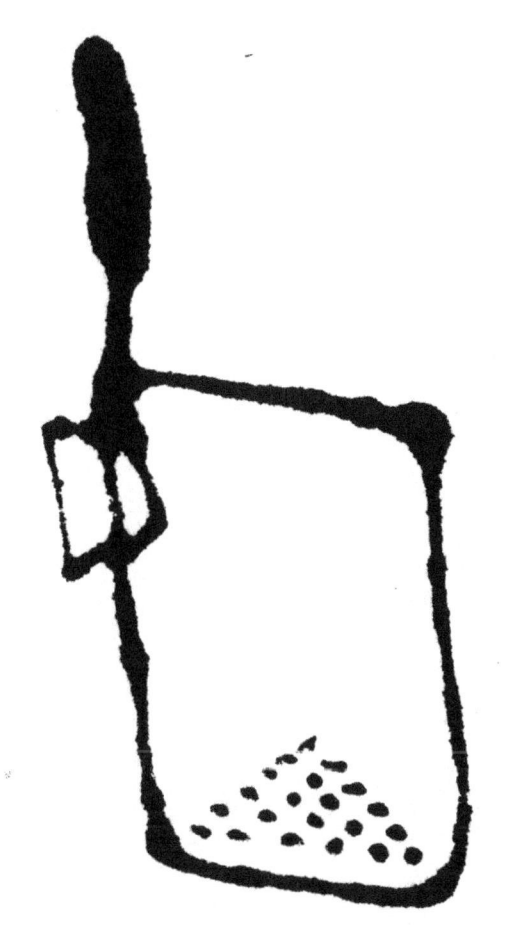

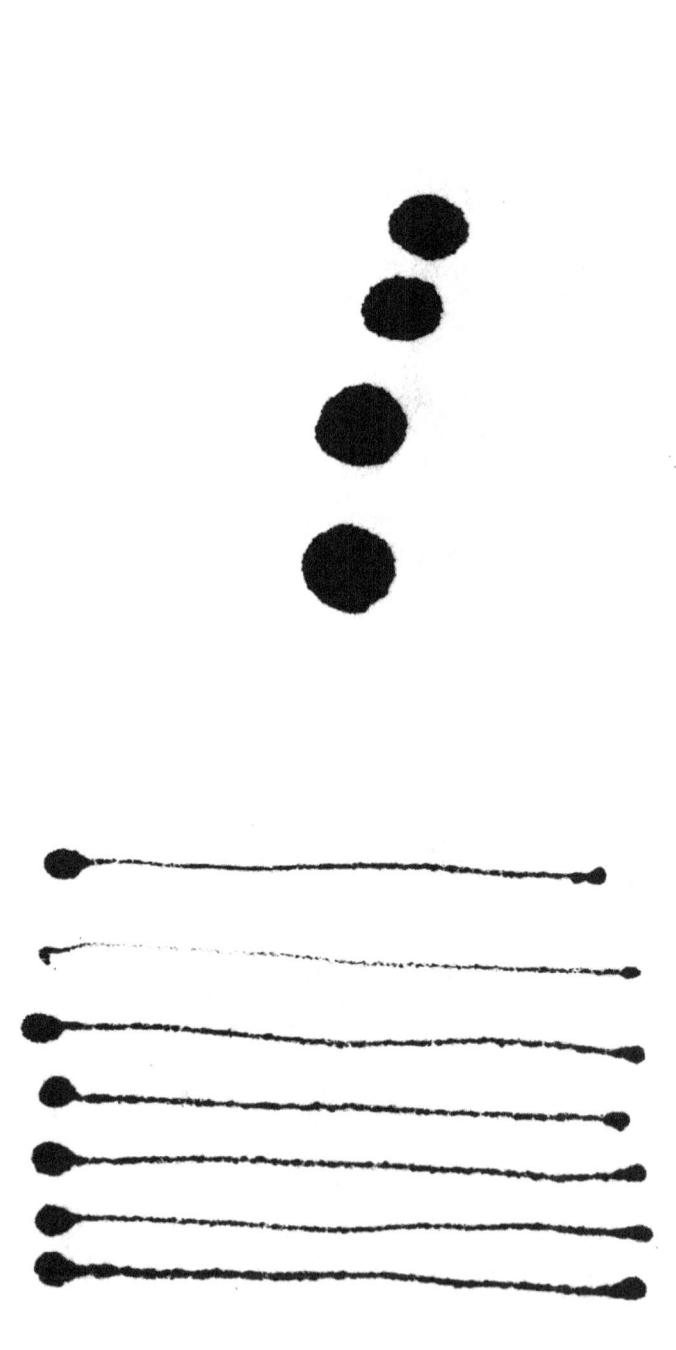

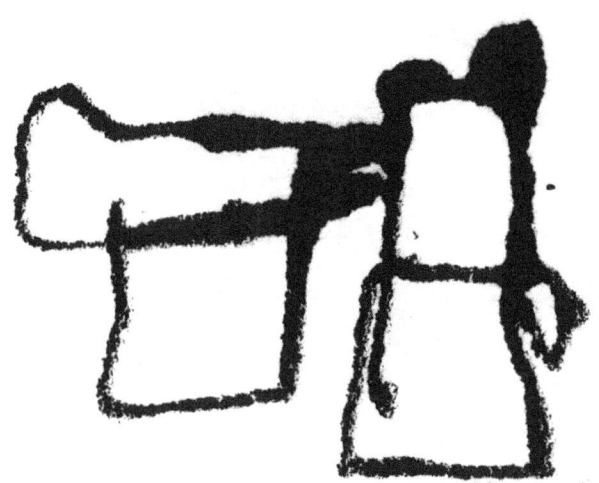

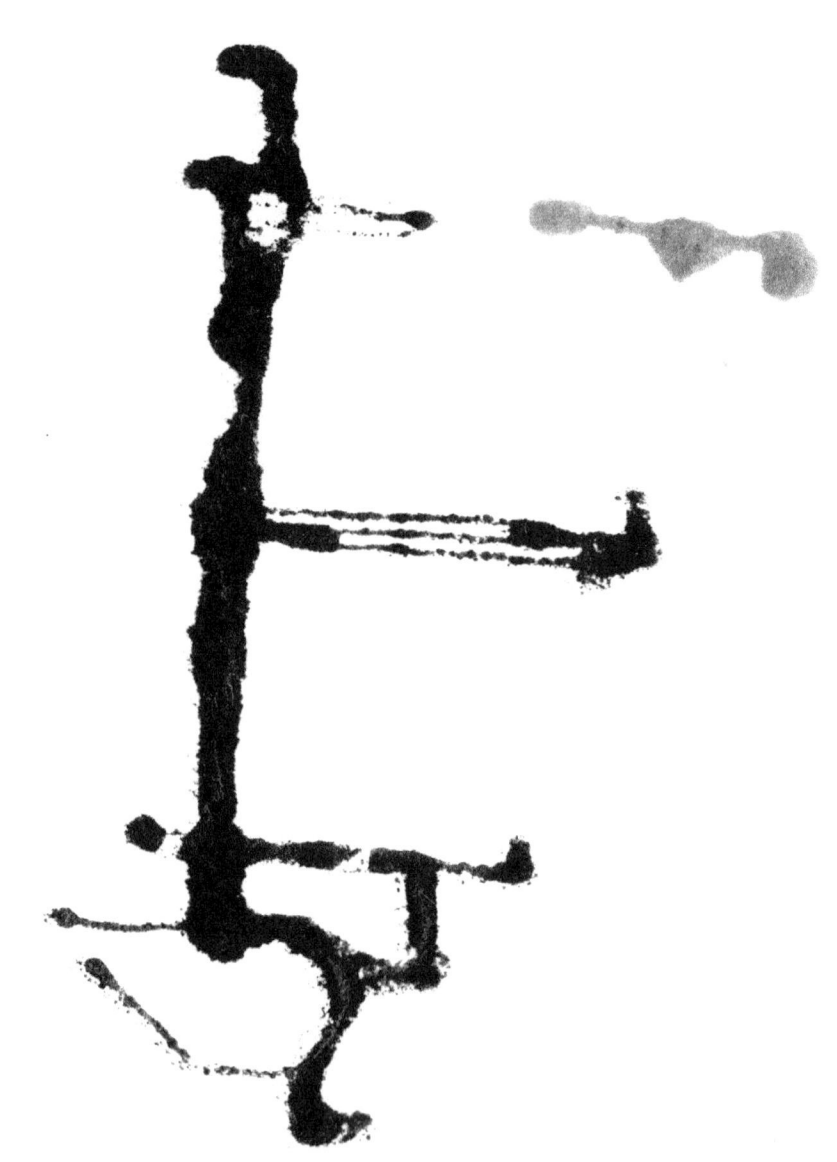

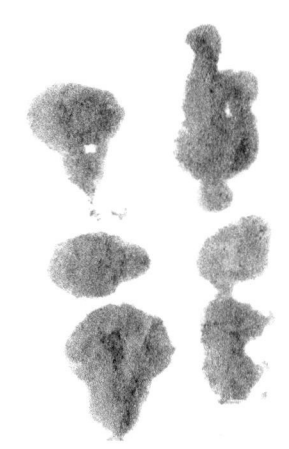

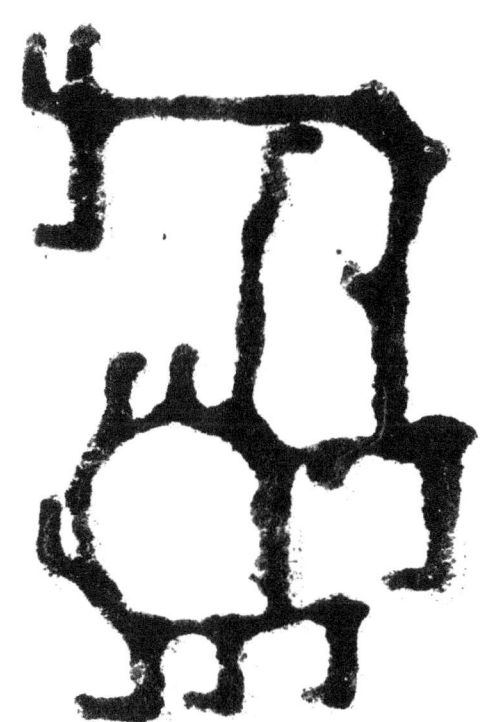

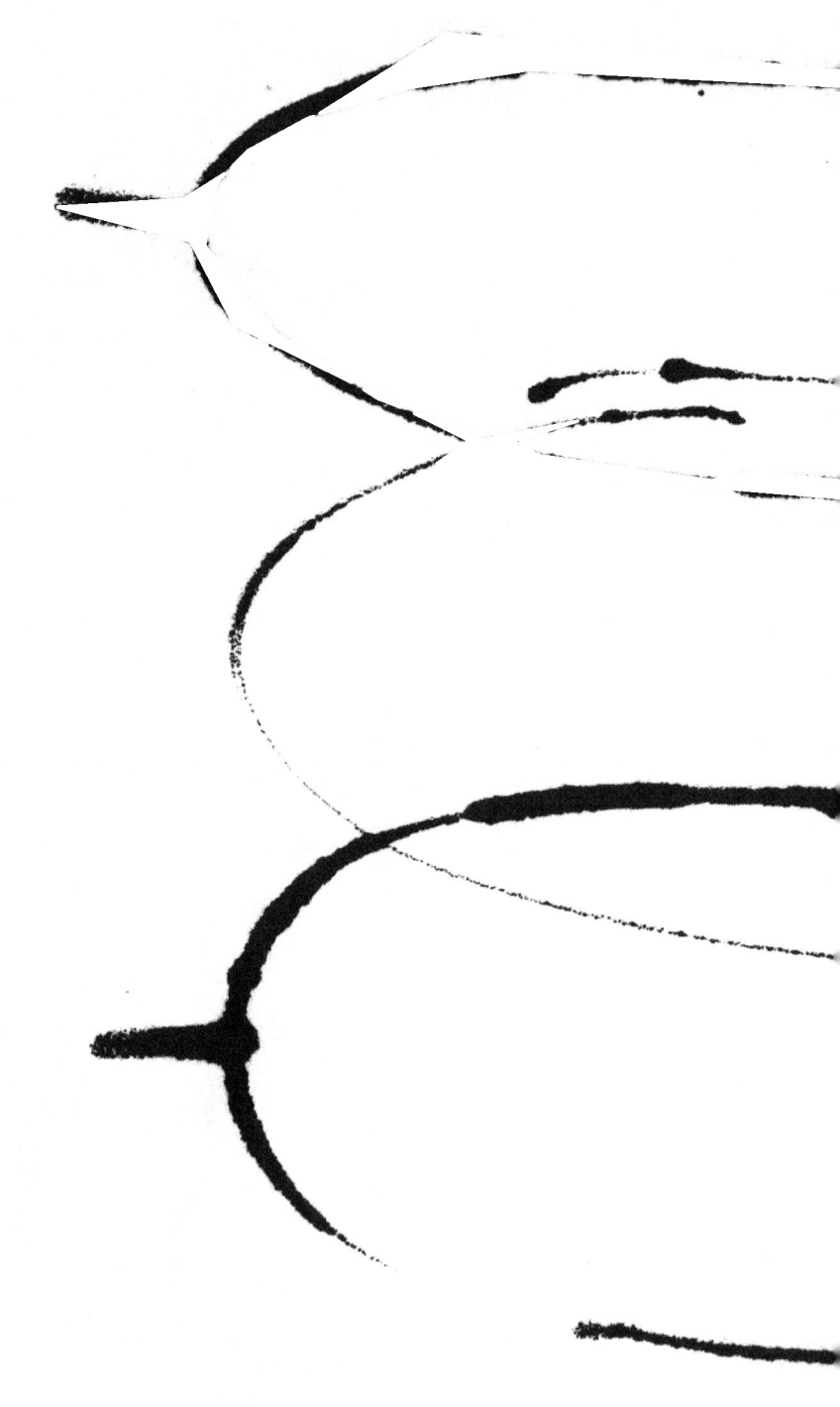

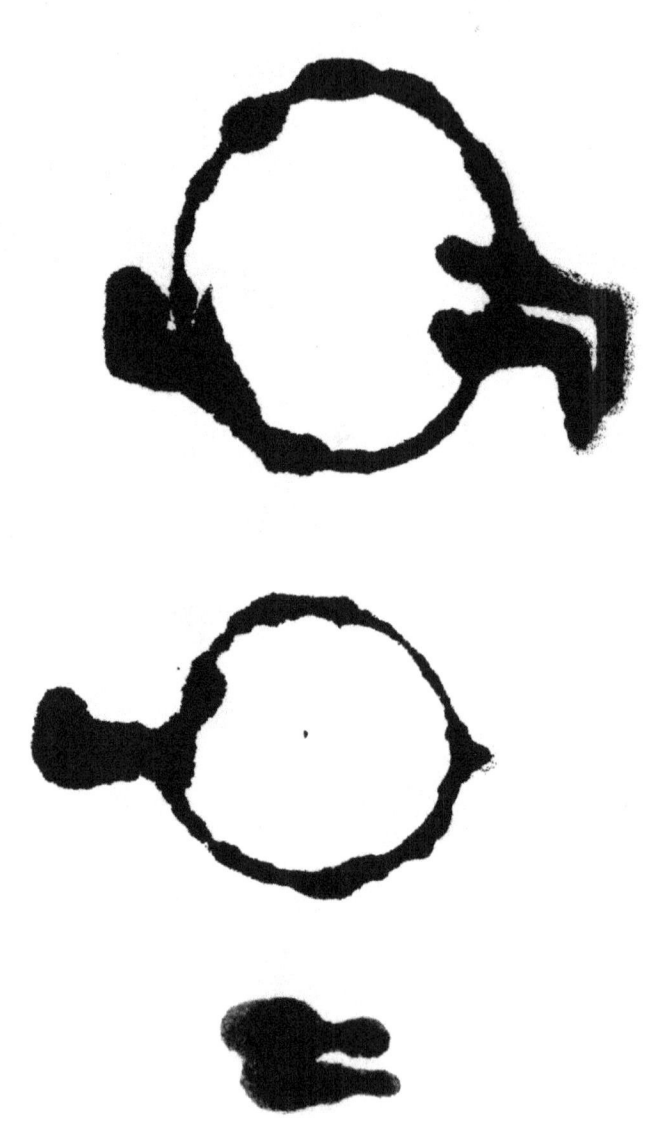

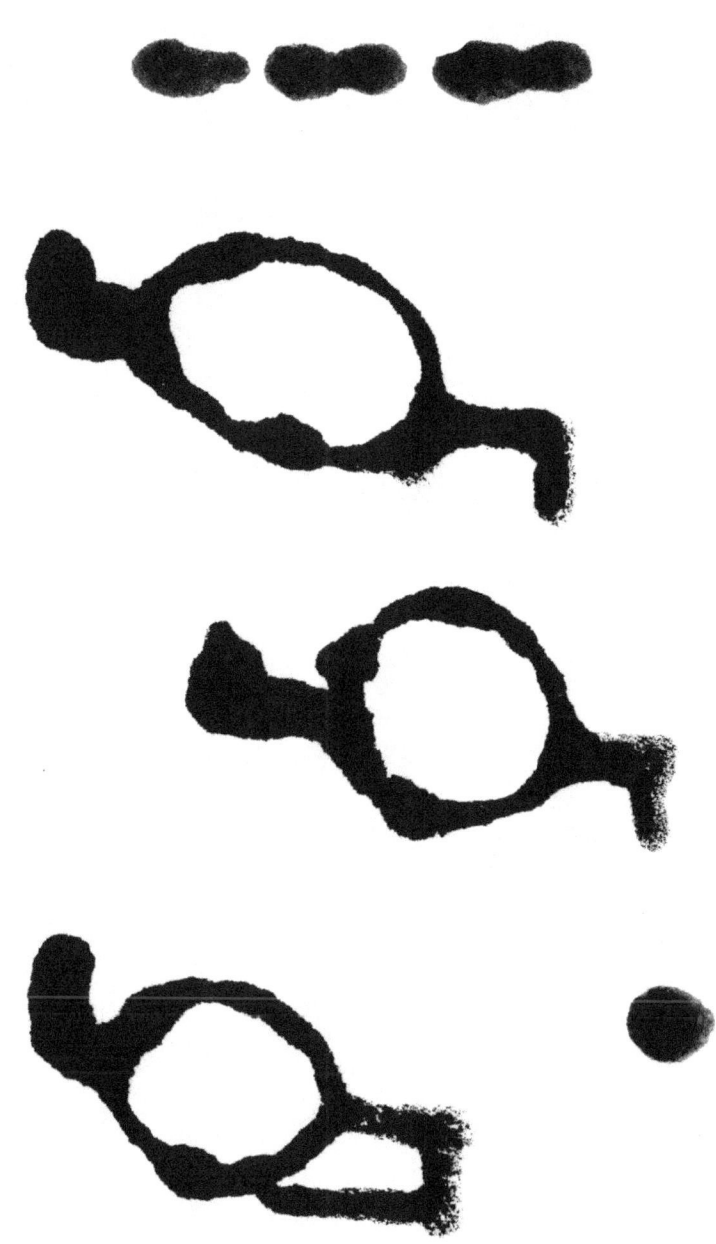

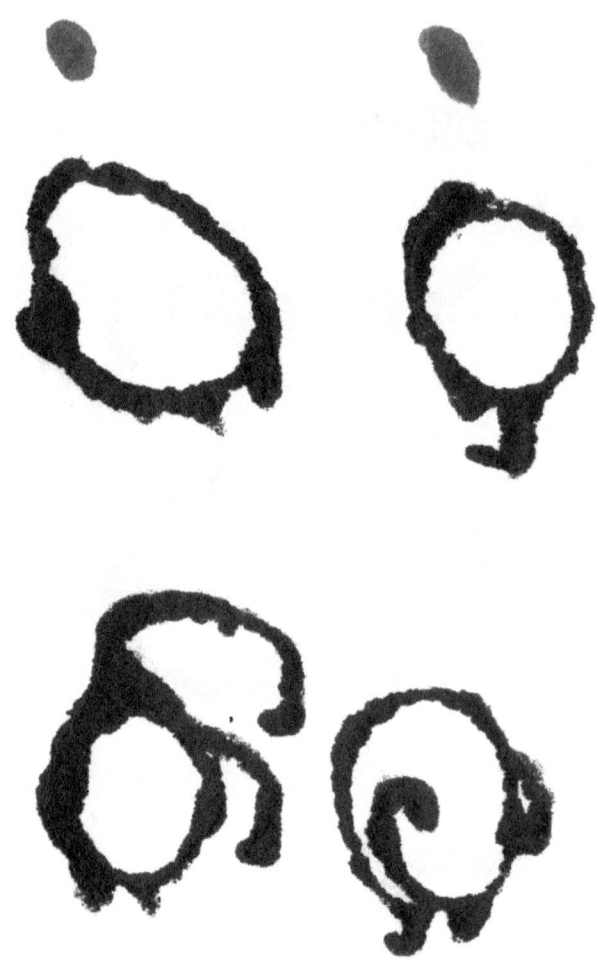

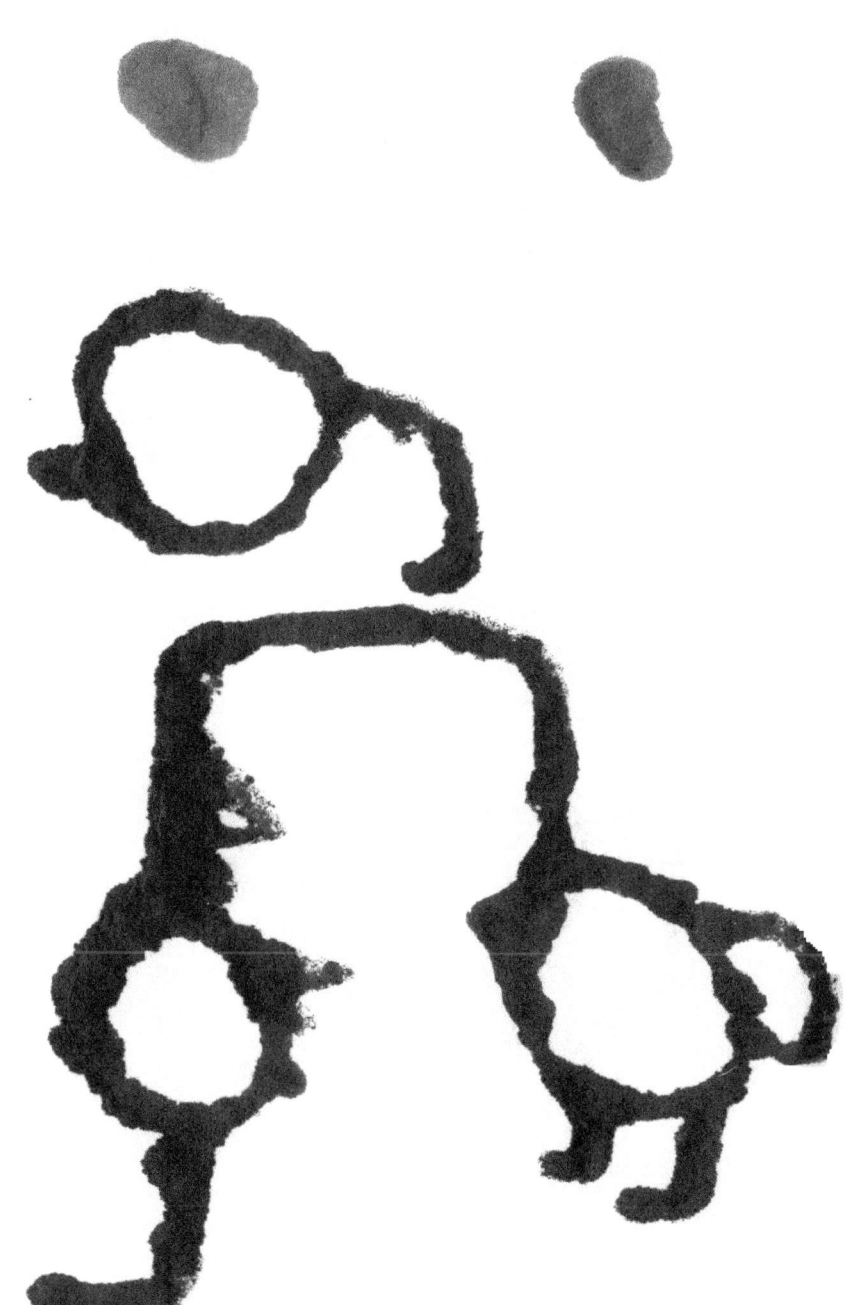

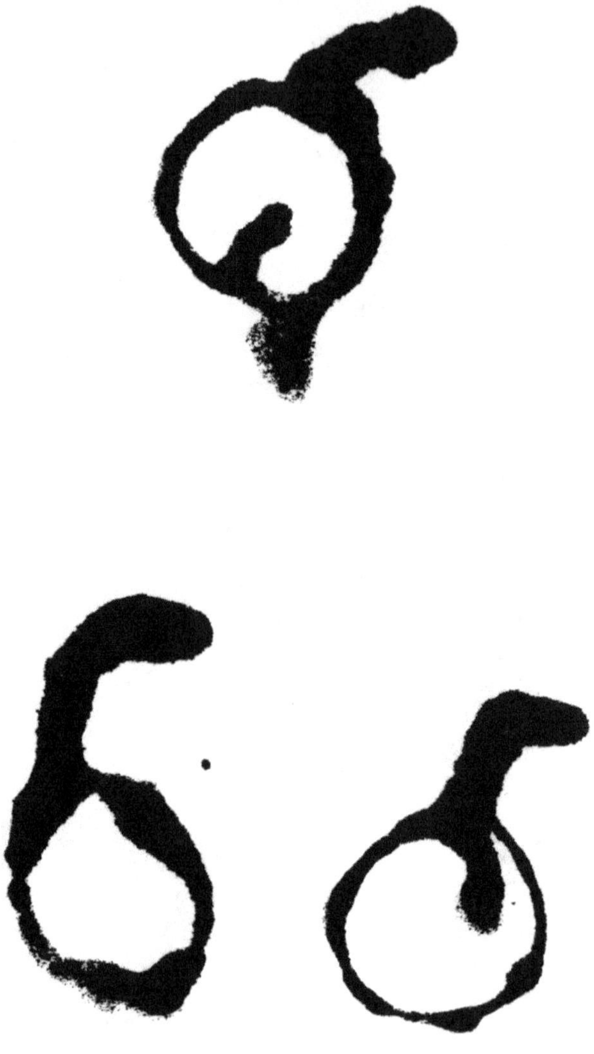

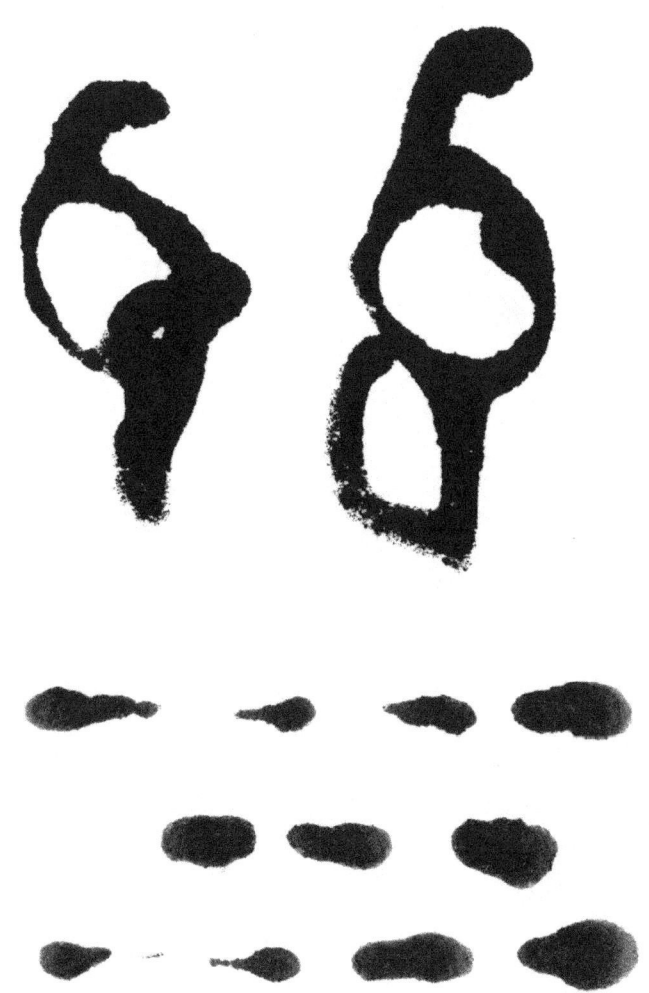

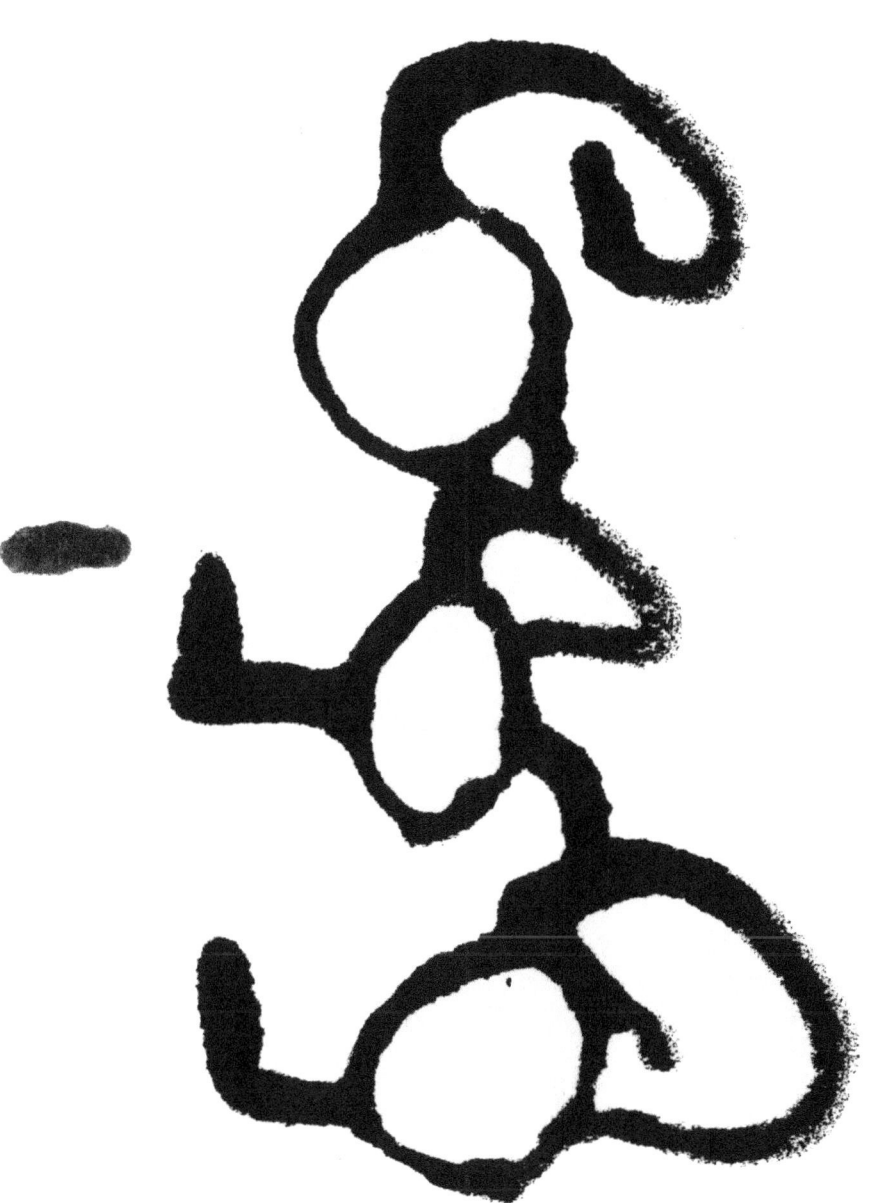

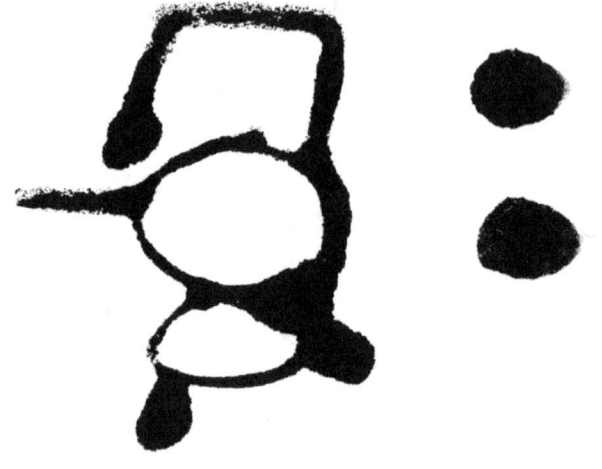
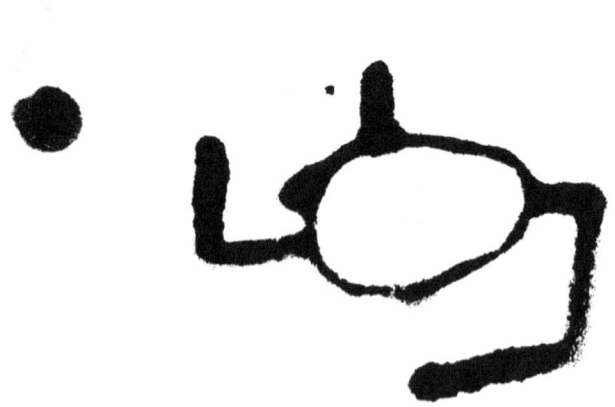

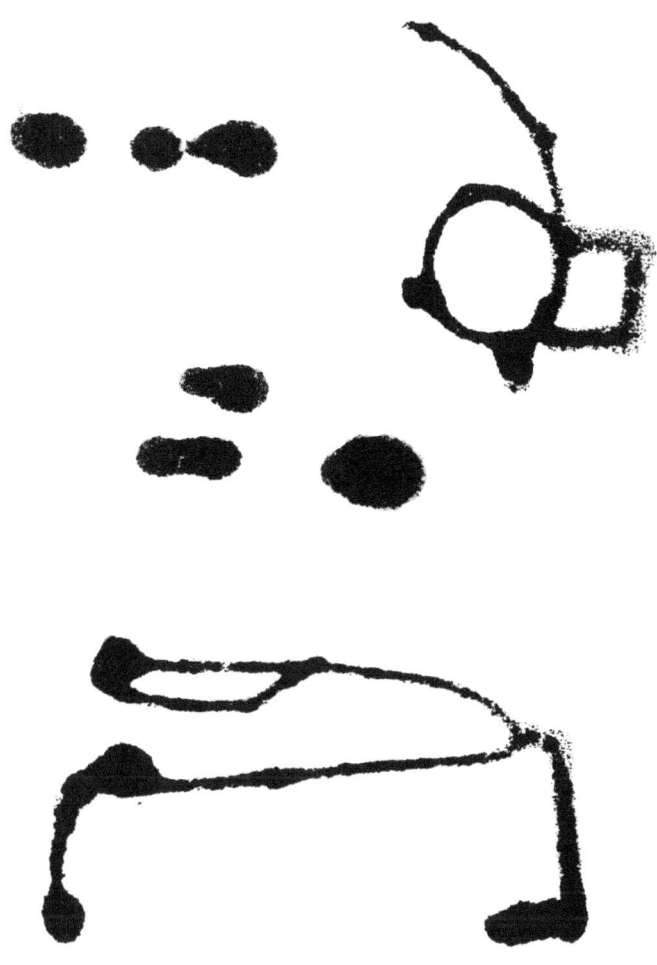

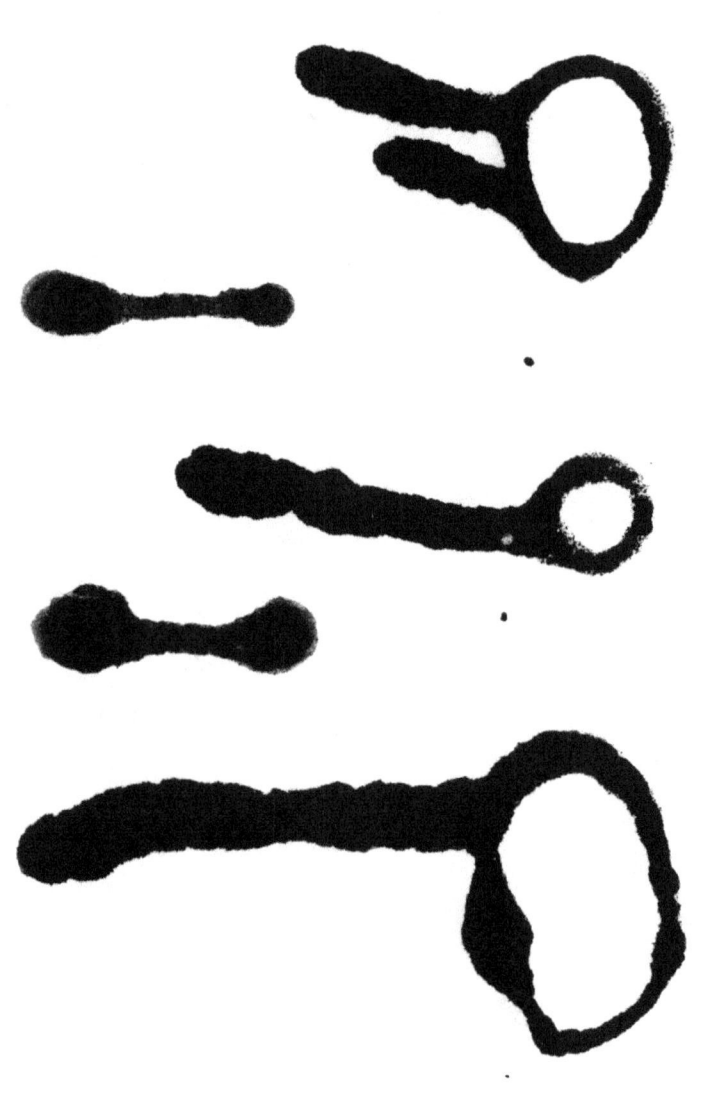

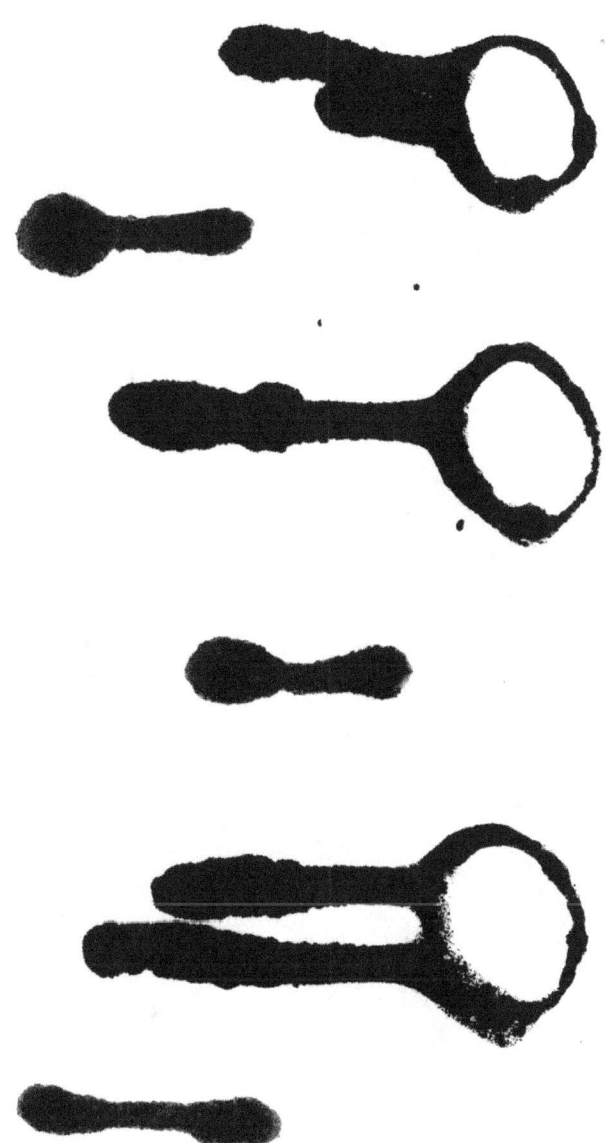

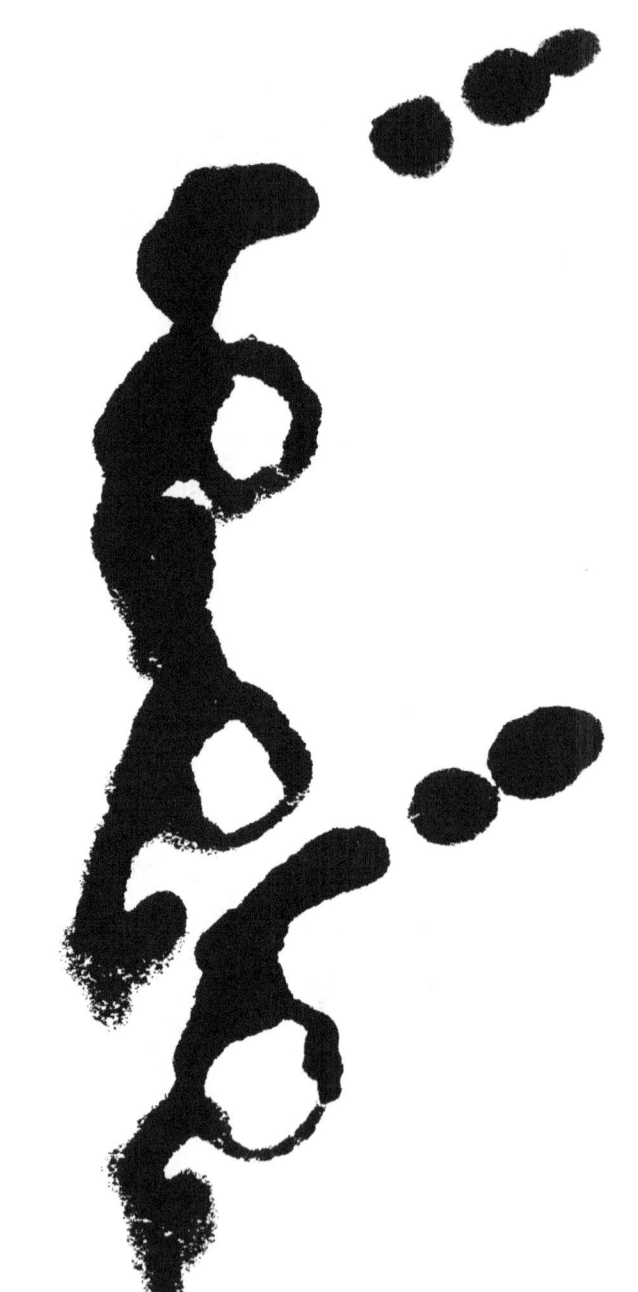

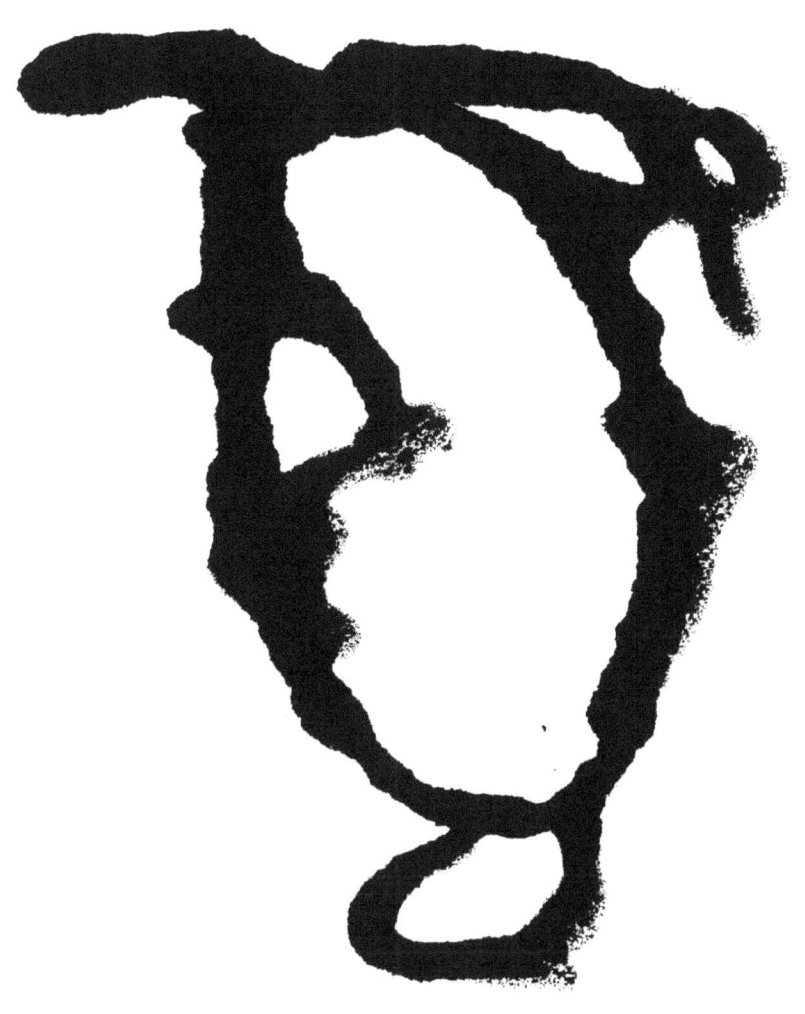

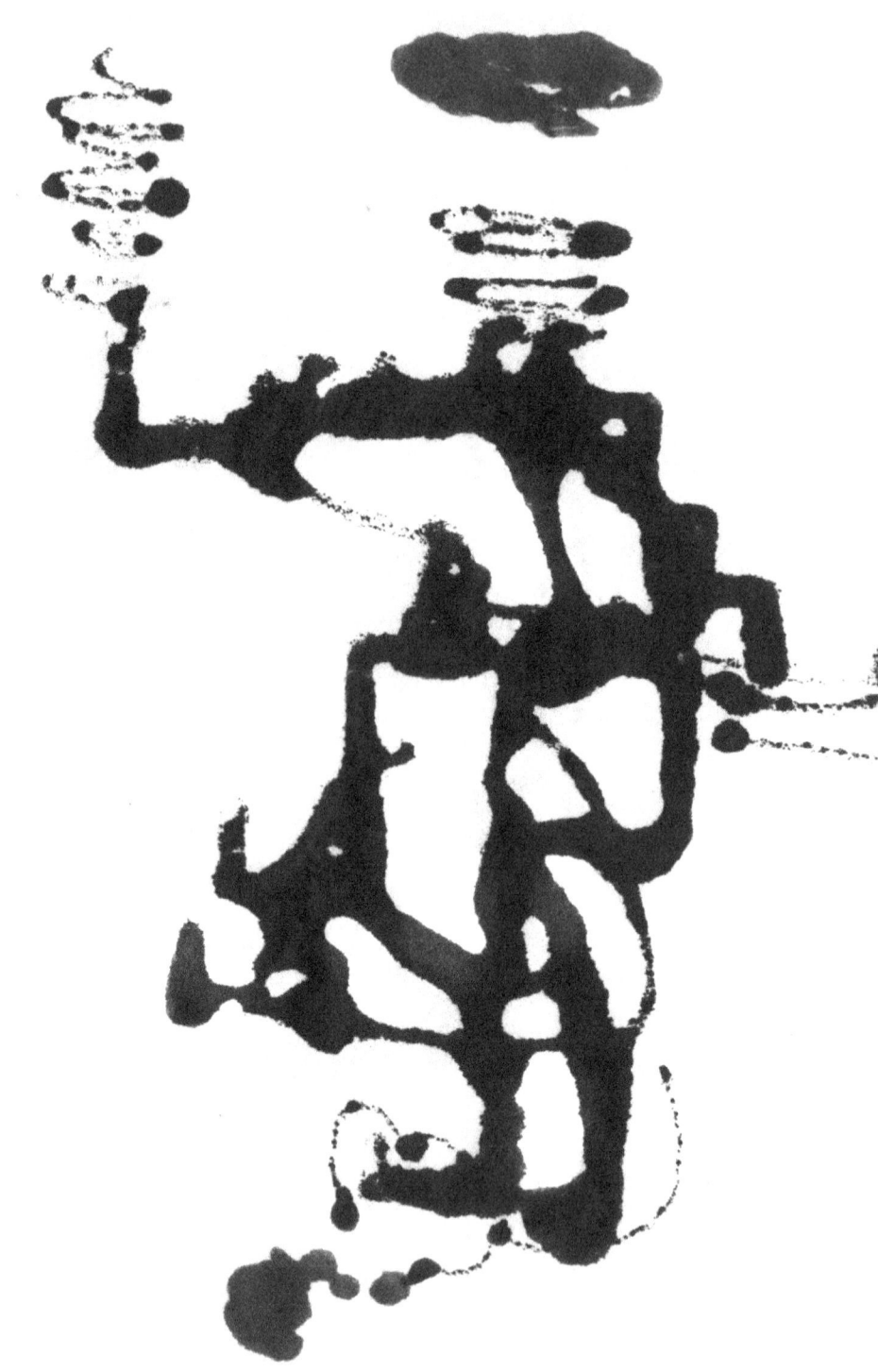

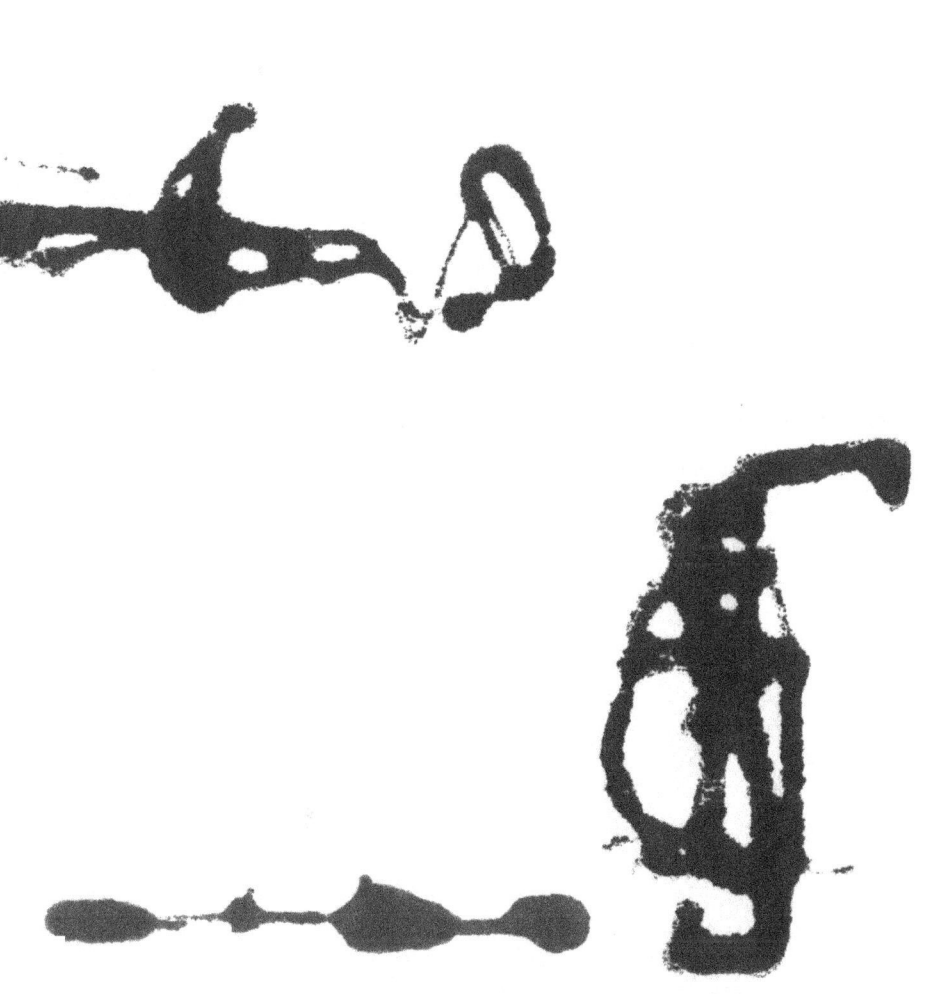

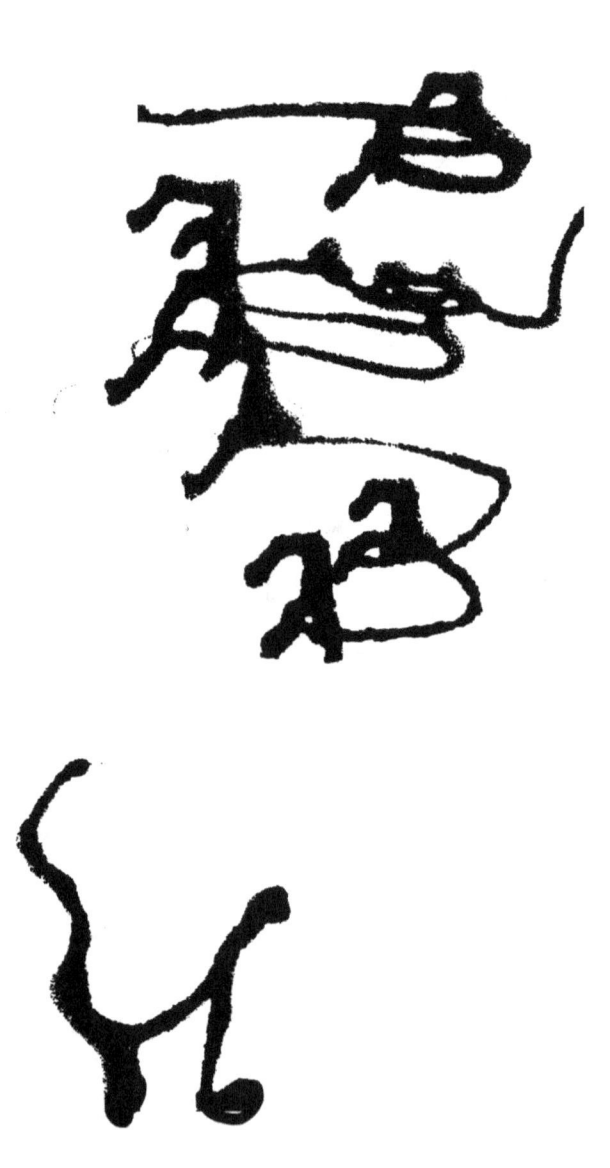

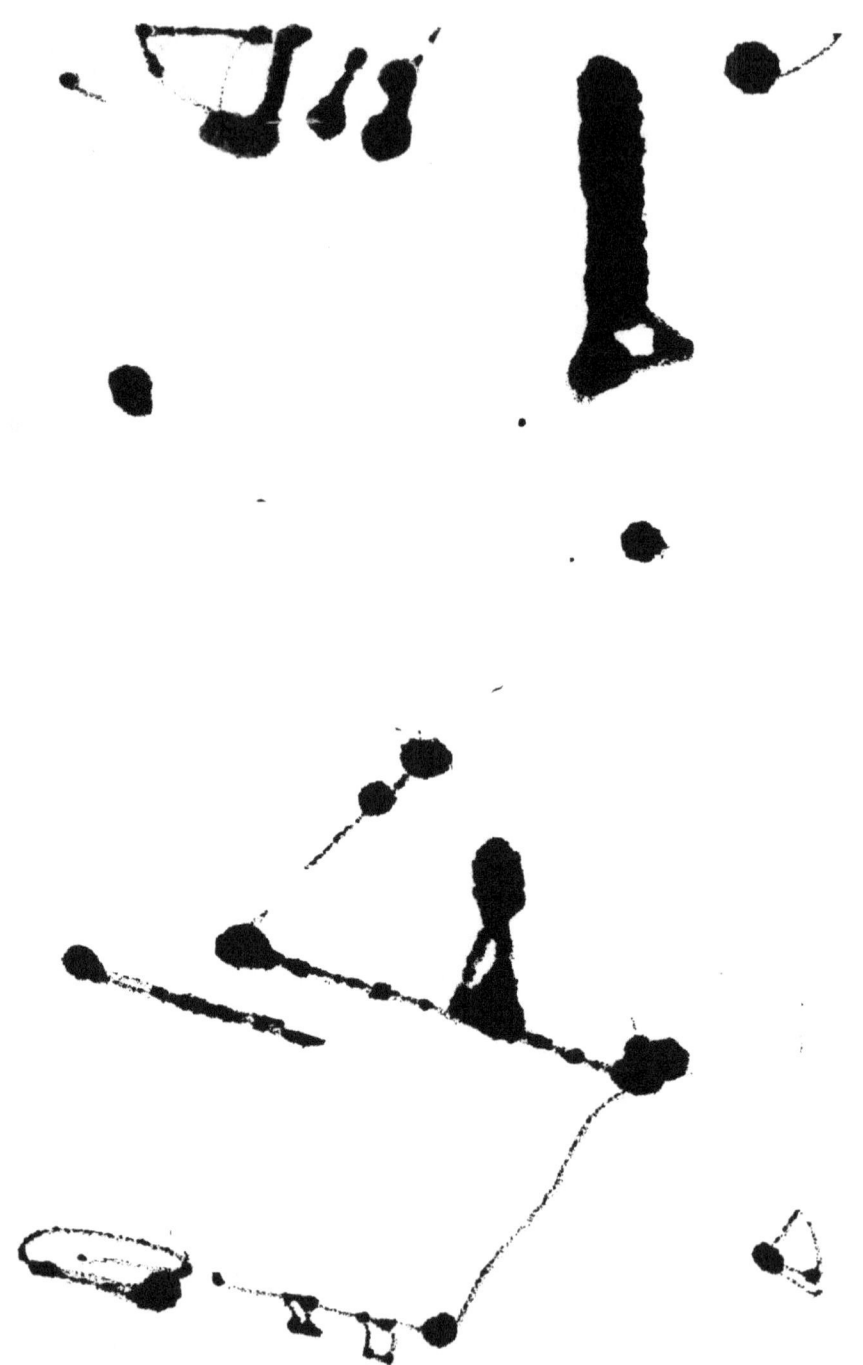

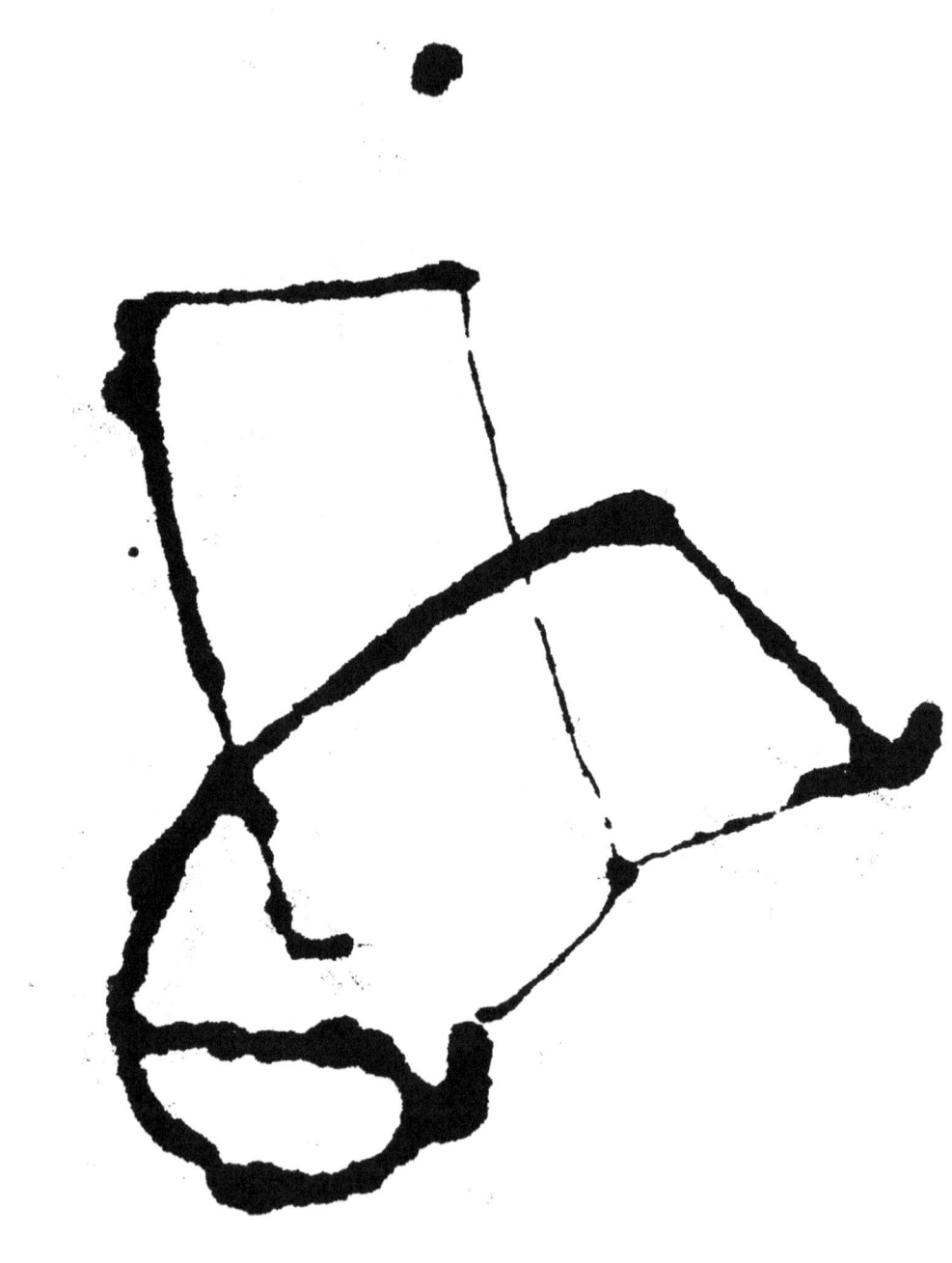

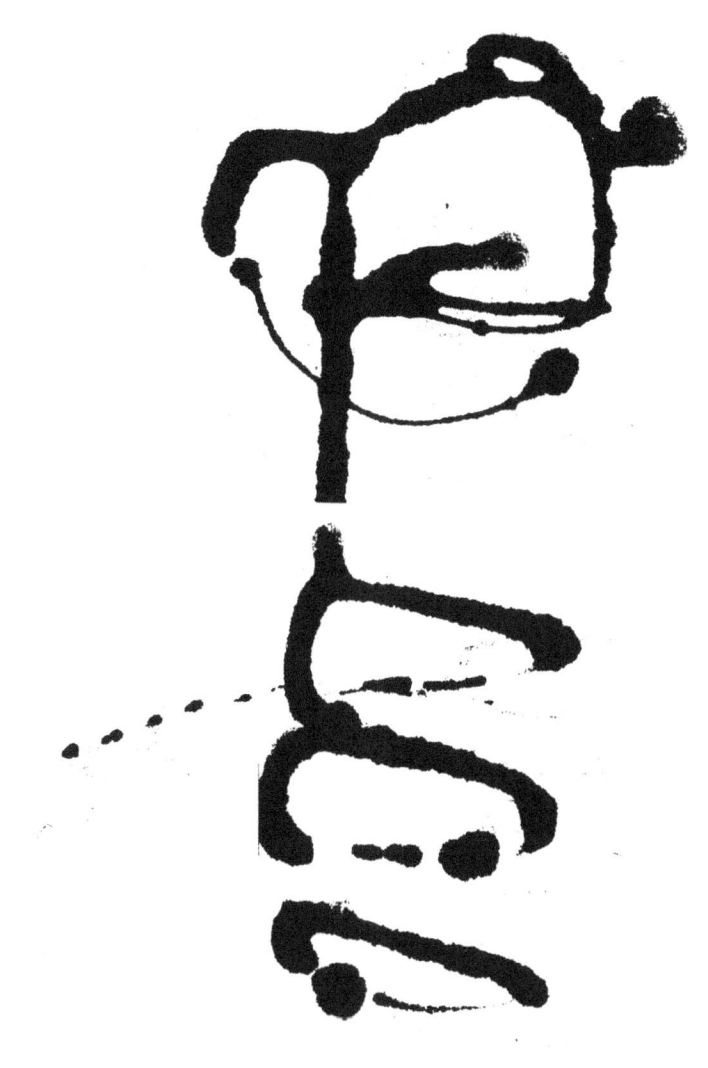

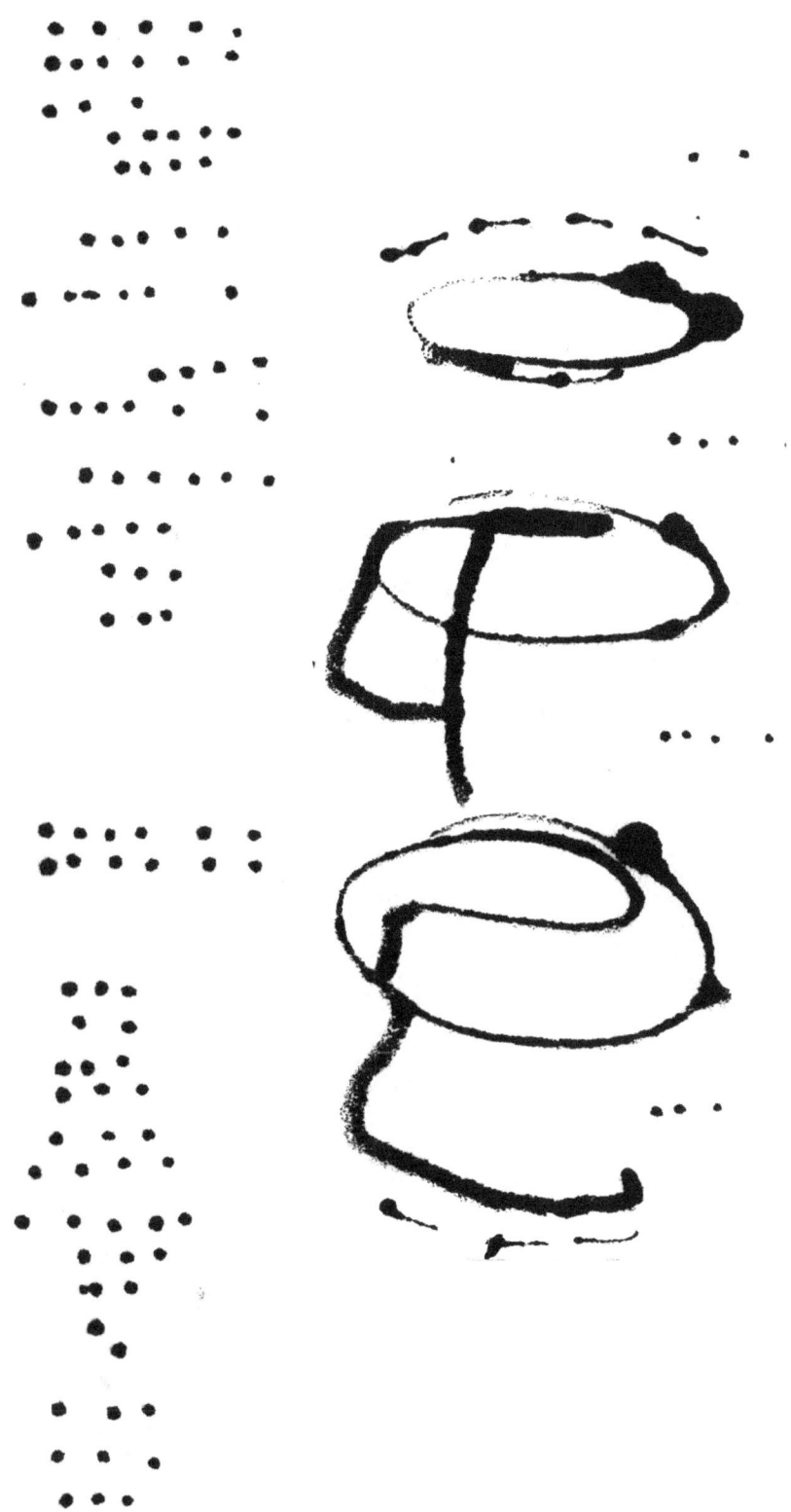

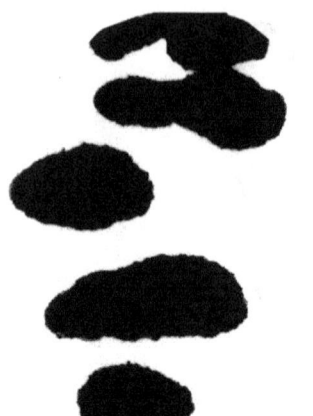

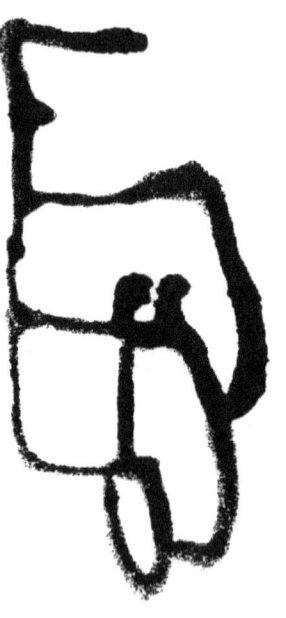

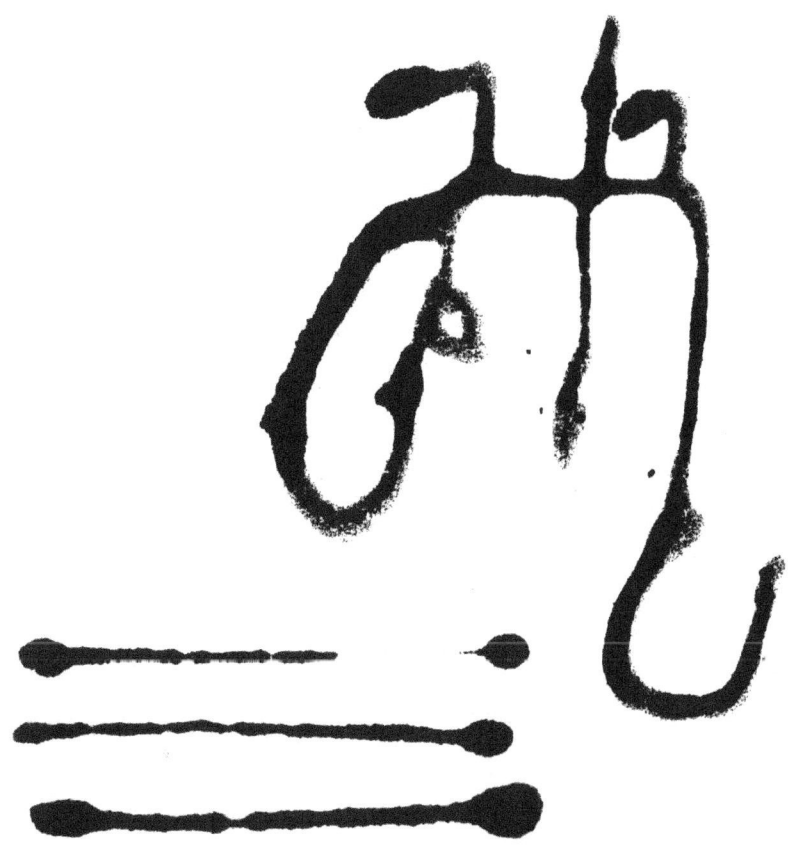

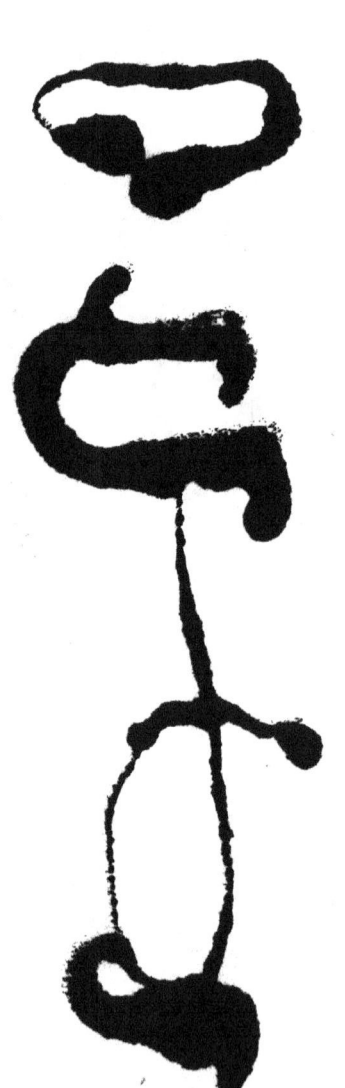

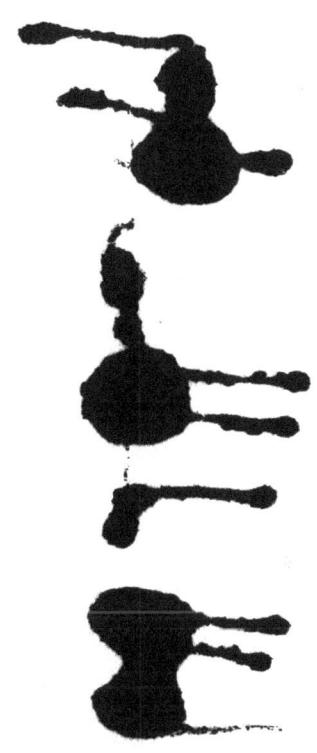

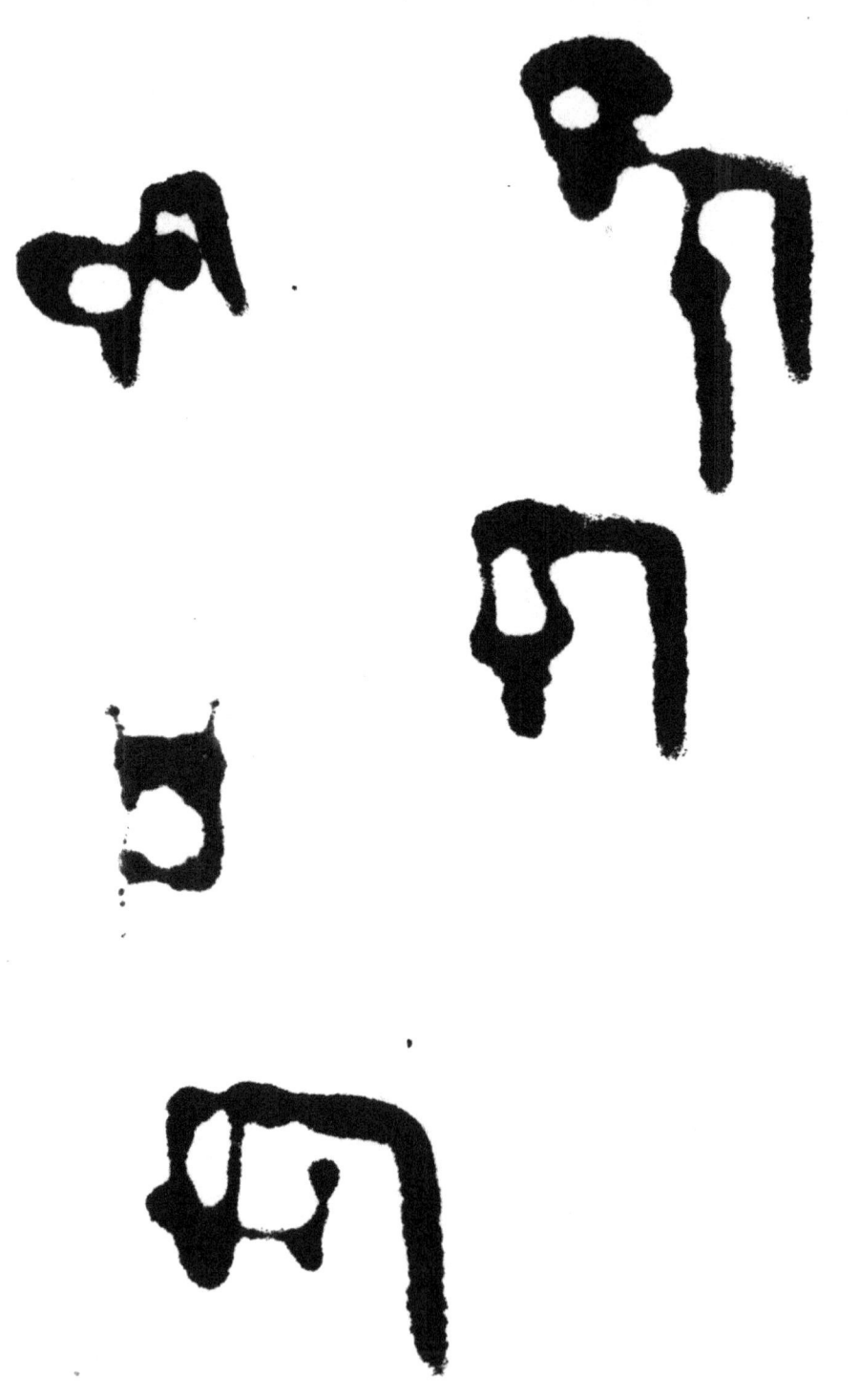

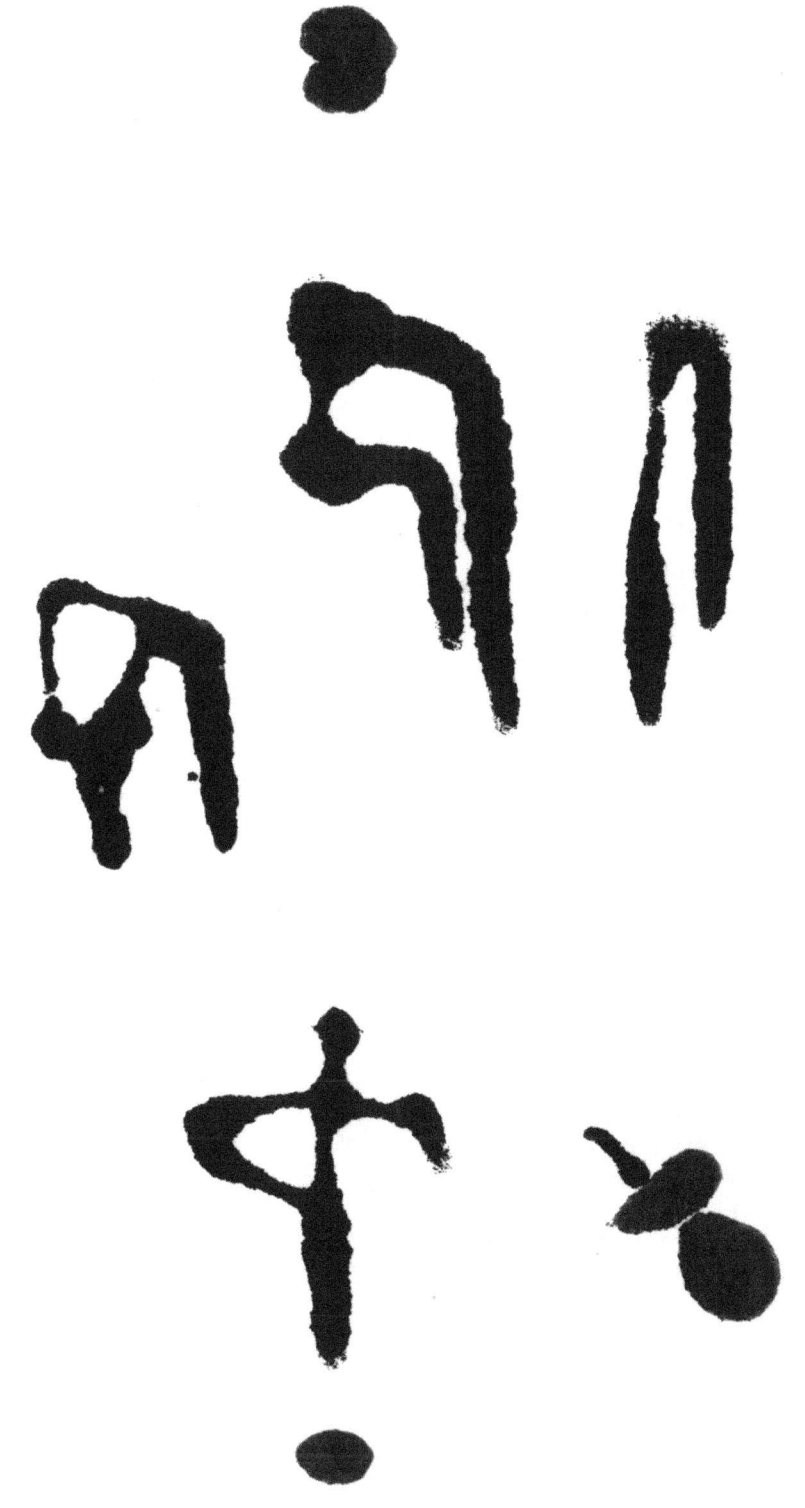

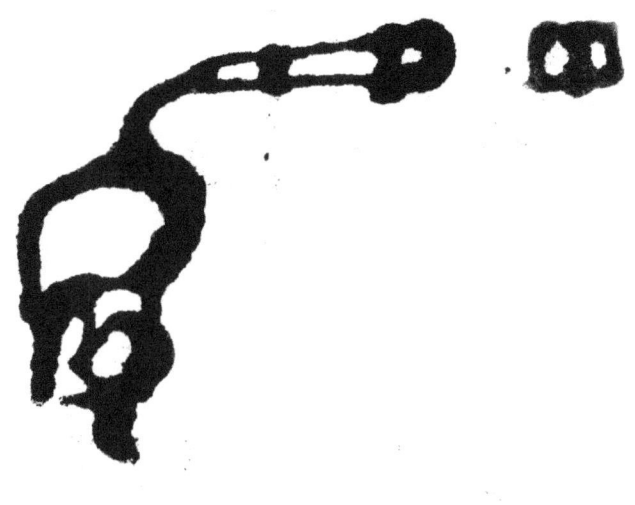

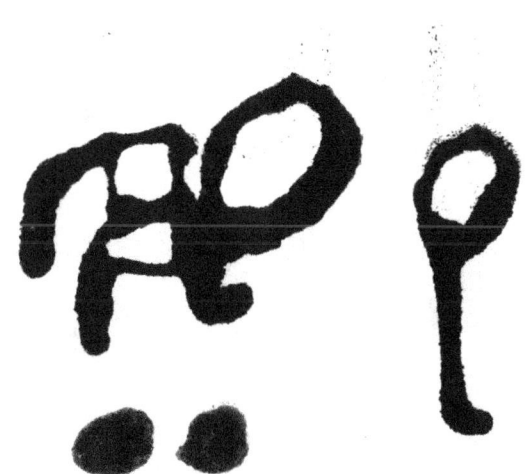

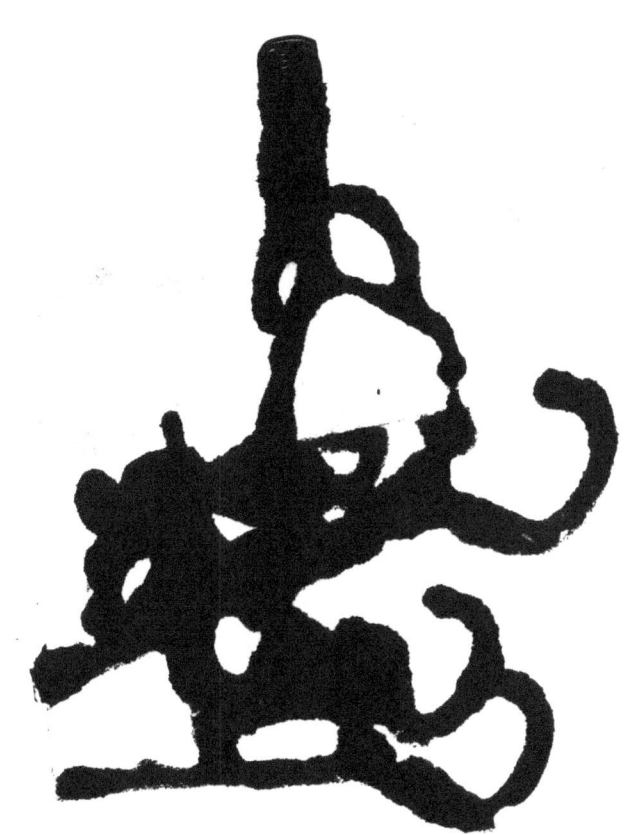

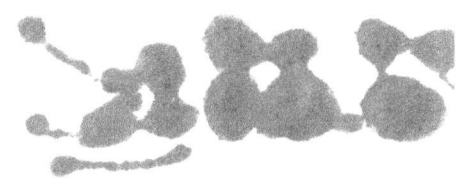

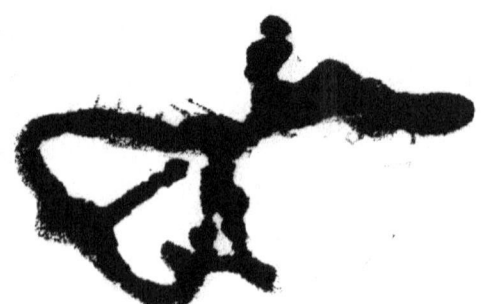

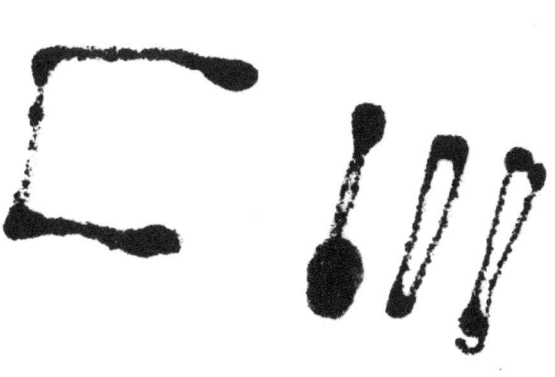

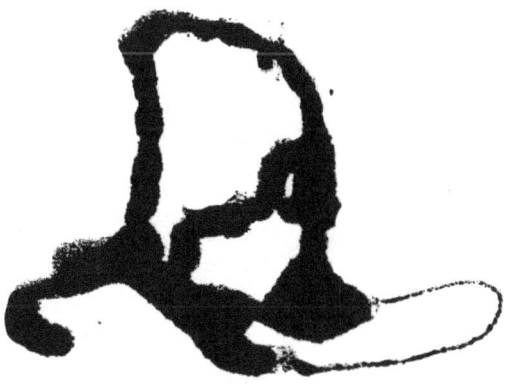

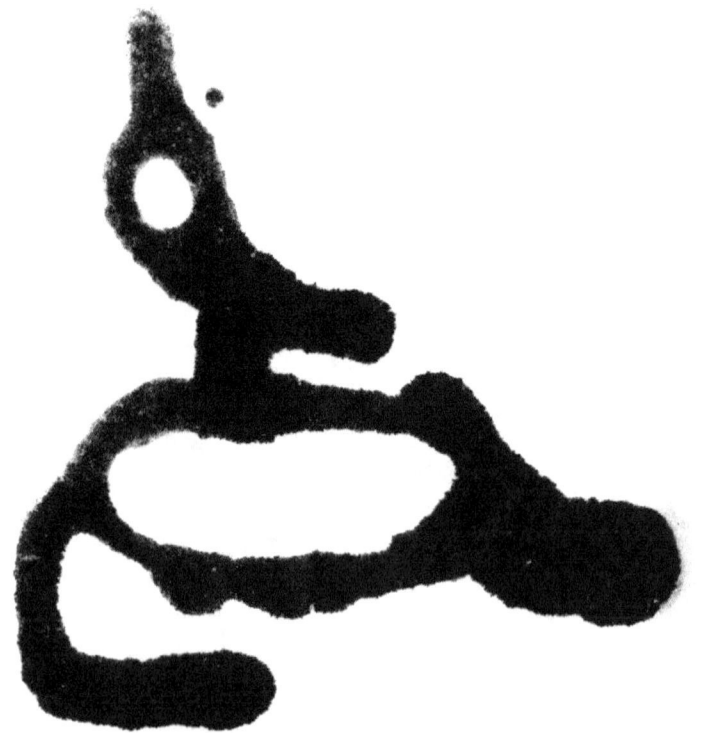

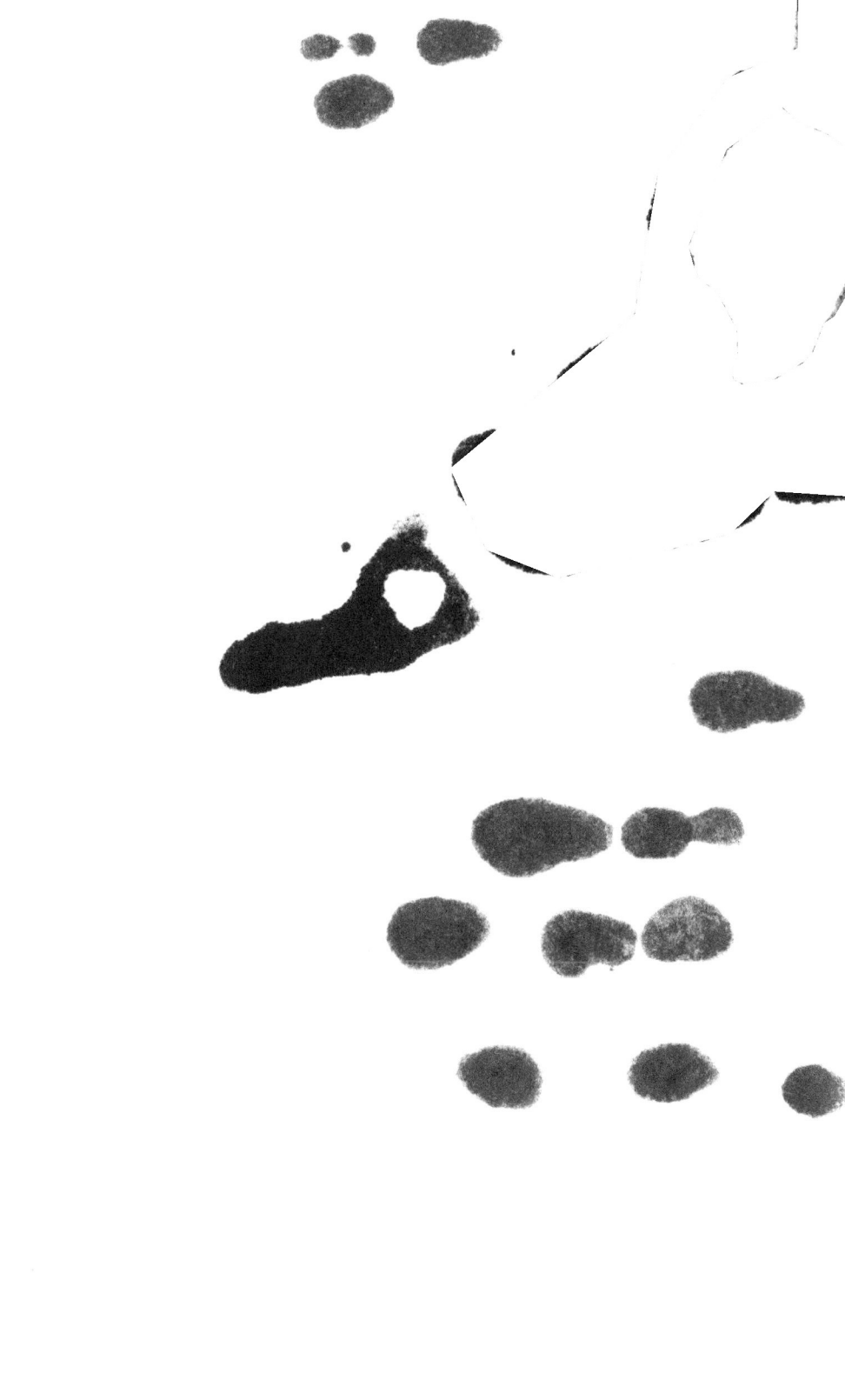

168.

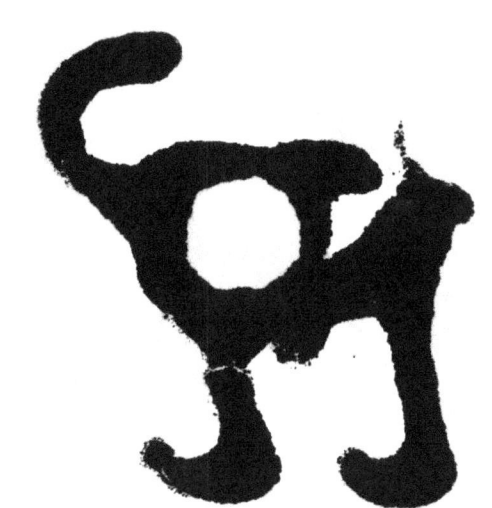

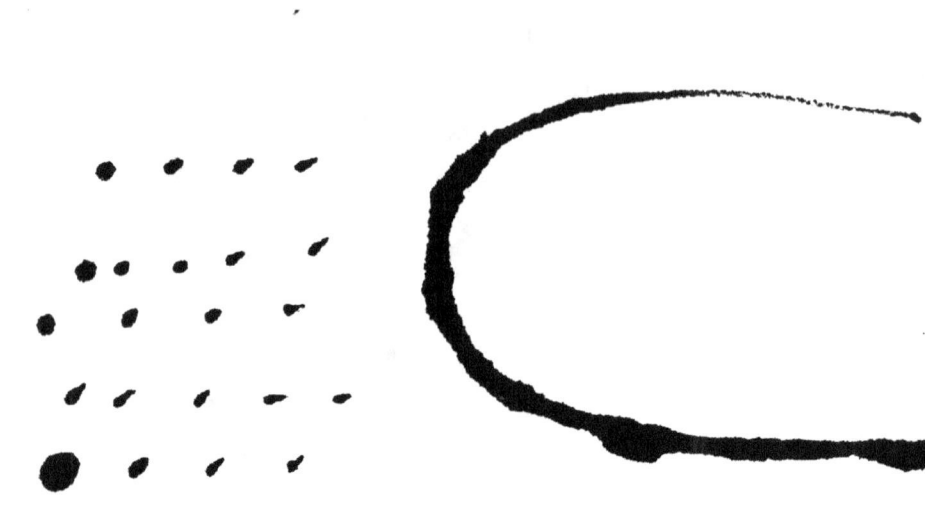

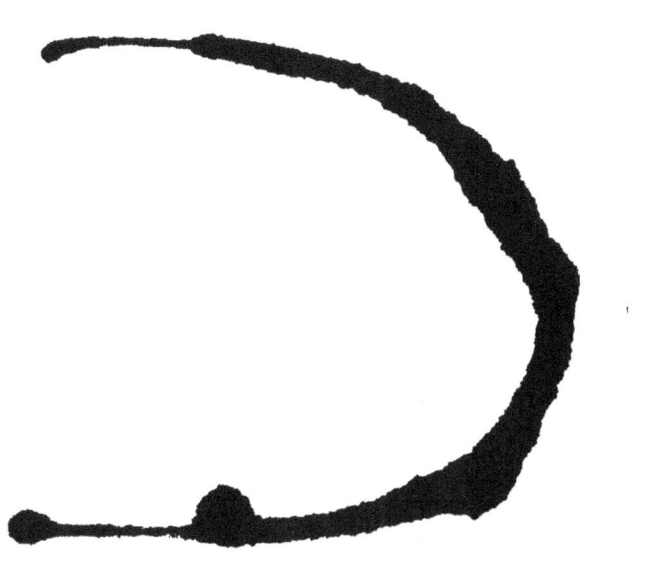

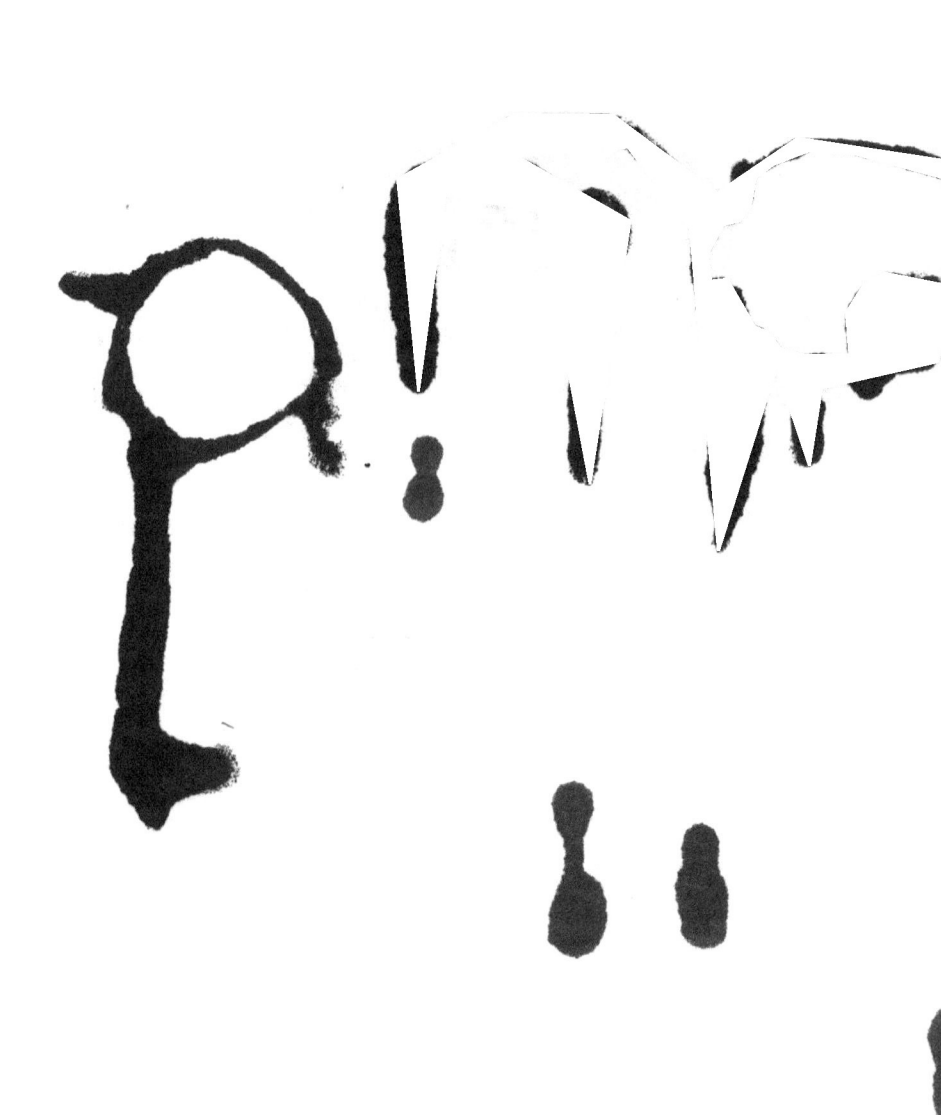

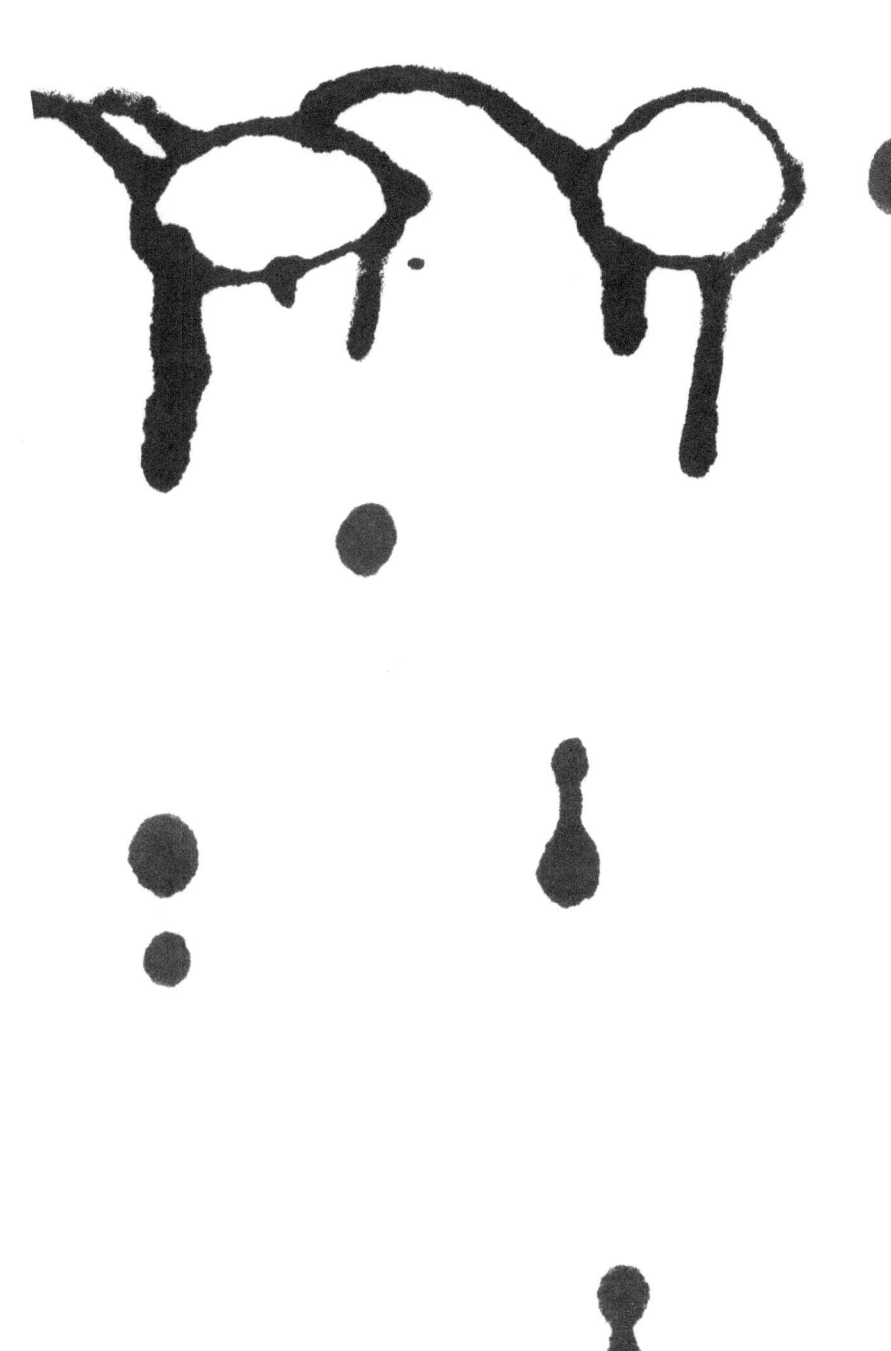

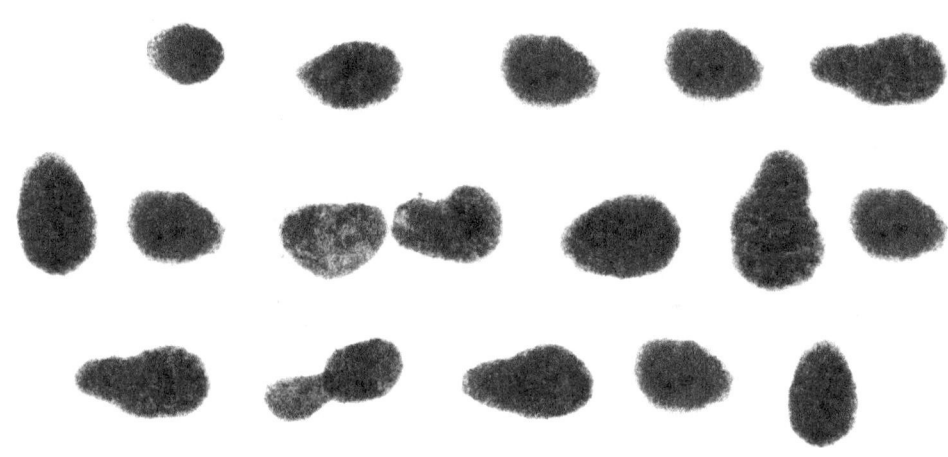

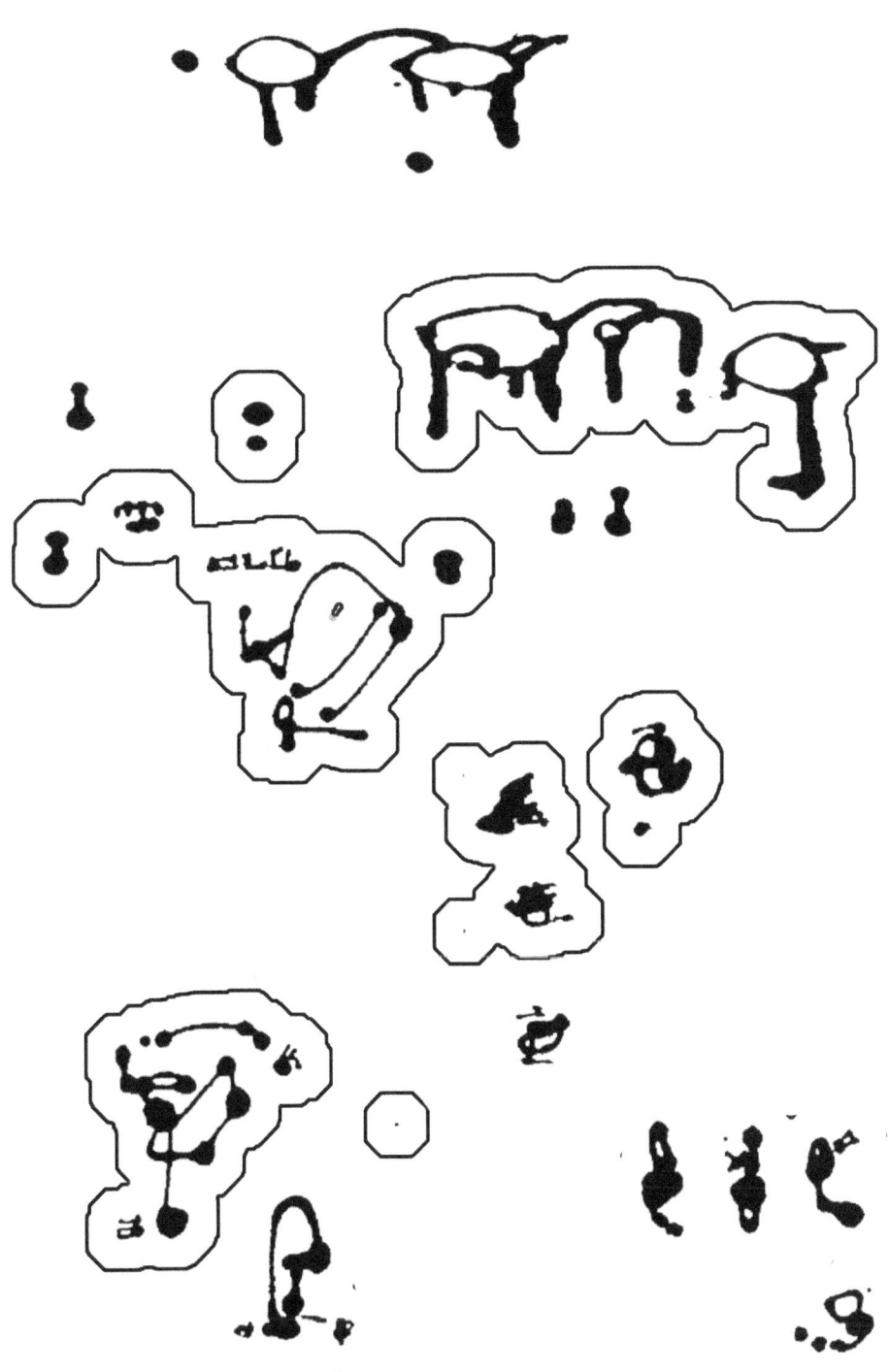

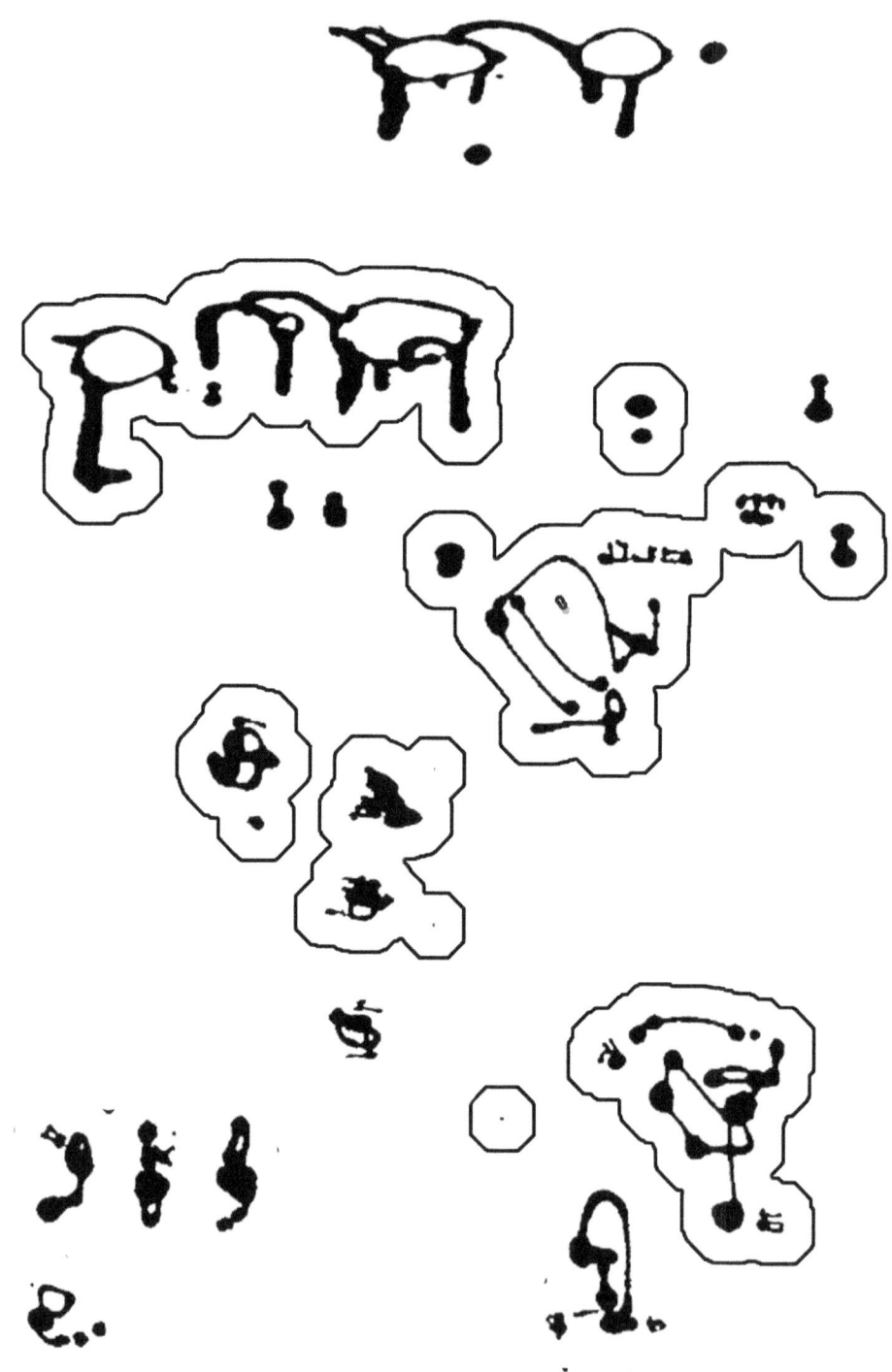

www.ingramcontent.com/pod-product-compliance
Lightning Source LLC
Chambersburg PA
CBHW070330190526
45169CB00005B/1823